WHEN GIANTS FALL

Overcoming Failure to Lead a Life of Integrity

Randy Spleth

Warner Press, Inc.
Warner Press and "Warner Press" logo are trademarks of Warner Press, Inc.

When Giants Fall
Written by Randall U. Spleth

Copyright ©2014 Randall U. Spleth
All rights reserved.

Cover and layout copyright ©2017 Warner Press Inc

Scripture quotations used in this book were taken from the following:

New International Version - Holy Bible, New International Version®, NIV® Copyright © 1973, 1978, 1984, 2011 by Biblica, Inc.® All rights reserved worldwide.

(NIV1984) - Scripture taken from HOLY BIBLE, NEW INTERNATIONAL VERSION®. NIV®. Copyright © 1973, 1978, 1984 by International Bible Society. Used by permission of Zondervan Publishing House. All rights reserved.

New Revised Standard Version Bible, copyright © 1989 the Division of Christian Education of the National Council of the Churches of Christ in the United States of America. Used by permission. All rights reserved.

All rights reserved. No part of this publication may be reproduced, stored in a retrieval system, or transmitted in any form or by any means—electronic, mechanical, photocopy, recording, or any other—except for brief quotations in printed reviews, without the prior permission of the publisher.

Requests for information should be sent to:

Warner Press Inc.
2902 Enterprise Dr.
P.O. Box 2499
Anderson, IN 46013
www.warnerpress.org

Editor: Karen Rhodes
Cover: Curtis Corzine
Layout: Katie Miller

ISBN: 9781593179410
This book is also available in e-book format.
Printed in USA

TABLE OF CONTENTS

Introduction 5

1. **What God Saw in David's Heart** 7
   (1 Samuel 16:1–13a)

2. **Courage to Face Giants** 15
   (1 Samuel 17:31–37, 48–49)

3. **Faithful Love** 25
   (1 Samuel 20:12-17)

4. **Doubting and Trusting God** 33
   (1 Samuel 21; 22:1a)

5. **Mercy vs. Revenge** 43
   (1 Samuel 26:21–25)

6. **God's Promise Fulfilled** 51
   (2 Samuel 5:1-13)

7. **Passions, Good and Bad** 59
   (2 Samuel 6)

8. **The Trap of Self-Righteousness** 69
   (2 Samuel 11:26—12:7a, 13b)

9. **Like Father, Like Son—But Worse!** 79
   (2 Samuel 13:1–2, 6–8, 11–16, 28; 14:28–33)

10. **Paralyzed by Grief** 89
    (2 Samuel 18:9–15, 24, 31–33)

11. **What David Saw in God's Heart** 99
    (2 Samuel 23:1–5a)

12. **If David's Story Ended Here** 109
    (1 Kings 2:1–12)

INTRODUCTION

Occasionally, I get sucked into a story whose characters, settings, and problems are so true to life that it becomes a part of my own. Such a story can change the way I perceive myself and the world around me. It can even change who I am.

King David of Israel found himself ensnared in such a story. He had committed adultery with the wife of a loyal warrior, a man so loyal that he accepted a suicide mission from the king, leaving his pregnant wife to marry her paramour. That could have been the end of it, except for a prophet who gained an audience with the king to tell him a story.

His narrative described a greedy sheep rancher who was not satisfied with his own flock, but connived to steal a lamb from his poor neighbor. The storyteller painted such a realistic picture that he pulled David into it, and the king demanded to know what kind of man would do such a dastardly thing. "You," the prophet said, "you are the man." The truth of the story cut to David's heart, and he repented in abject sorrow.

Bible stories have just as much romance, intrigue, treachery, and murder as the best-selling "beach reads" that tourists tote on their summer vacations, but their purpose is more than mere entertainment. The stories of Scripture describe our human condition with painful authenticity. They reveal who we are and how we must change if we are to have enduring relationships with our neighbors and with God. So these stories are transformative. You may be amused, appalled, or scandalized as you read them—but you will also be changed. That's why they are in the Bible.

I invite you to read and reflect on the entire story of David's life. As you do, I pray that David's story will become part of your own.

Randy Spleth
Indianapolis, Indiana

WHAT GOD SAW IN DAVID'S HEART
1 Samuel 16:1–13

Among the men of the Bible, David is second only to Jesus. He shows up in more chapters of the Old Testament than anyone else and there are fifty-nine references to David in the New Testament. He was a man of great courage, devotion, and loyalty. He was also a murderer, an adulterer, and an absentee father given to violence, with a willful disregard of God's Word. Despite this, David was described as "a man after [God's] own heart" (1 Samuel 13:14; Acts 13:22). David's story starts with an old judge, a lost herd of donkeys, a generation of one-eyed men, and a peculiar event that most of us would not imagine being in the Bible.

One thousand years before Jesus was born, a radical social experiment was underway in the Promised Land and it wasn't going well. The Bible says, "In those days there was no king in Israel; all the people did what was right in their own eyes" (Judges 21:25). Can you imagine living in such a society? People wantonly took advantage of one another. They stole, they cheated, they lied, they even murdered. They literally did as they pleased. The only recourse for justice was to appeal to a handful of respected leaders called the "judges" of Israel. The last judge was a man named Samuel—so old, overworked, and tired that he couldn't stop much of the lawlessness that was taking place. He certainly couldn't deal with the malicious behavior of "the neighbors."

"The neighbors" were the indigenous people we would call Palestinians today. When God handed the Promised Land over to Israel, it was "a land flowing with milk and honey, ...the country of the Canaanites, the Hittites, the Amorites, the Perizzites, the Hivites, and the Jebusites" (Exodus 3:8). This area was named Palestinia in the second century AD by the Roman government, but the names *Palestine* and *Palestinians* do not appear in Scripture. The Old King James version of the Bible translates the Hebrew word for Philistines as *Palestinians* in three different places, but that was a mistake. All of the current translations of Scripture, including the New King James Version, have corrected this historical slip. Even though the word *Palestinian* was unknown in Old Testament times, the conflict between Israelites and Palestinians dates to that time 1,400 years before the birth of Christ. In those days, Palestinians were simply called the Israelites' "neighbors" (Joshua 9:16–19).

An Ammonite King by the name of Nahash was terrorizing the people of God. He ordered his soldiers to find Israelite men and poke out their right eyes. So every Israelite man looked like a one-eyed pirate with a patch over the right eye. It was so bad that it felt like "no one was left of the Israelites across the Jordan whose right eye Nahash, king of the Ammonites, had not gouged out" (1 Samuel 10:27).

"WE WANT A KING"

So it should not have surprised the old judge Samuel when a group showed up and said, "Sam, something's got to be done. You're old; your boys are worthless. You've got no successor and we've got this big problem with this crazy Ammonite Nahash. We want a king" (1 Samuel 8:4–5).

It hurt Samuel's feelings. He felt rejected. *Samuel prayed to the LORD, and the LORD said to Samuel, "Listen to the voice of the people in all that they say to you; for they have not rejected you, but they have rejected me from being king over them"* (1 Samuel 8:6–7). Samuel finally relented and set out to find them a king.

A very rich man by the name of Kish of the small tribe of Benjamin had lost his donkeys and sent his son Saul to find them. The search wasn't going well so he decided to seek the help of Samuel. When Saul showed up, Samuel greeted him and said, "Stop looking for your donkeys; they are found and back home where they belong. Start looking for a kingdom because I'm going to anoint you the king of God's people" (1 Samuel 9:20).

Samuel told Saul to kneel because this young fellow was a foot taller than anyone else. *Samuel took a vial of oil and poured it on his head, and kissed him; he said, "The LORD has anointed you ruler over his people Israel. You shall reign over the people of the LORD and you will save them from the hand of their enemies all around"* (1 Samuel 10:1). When Saul stood up, the Bible says, *God gave him another heart* (1 Samuel 10:9).

On his way home to his father Kish and the lost donkeys, Saul fell into a prophetic trance and began to prophesy. Once home, he didn't accept his kingship but went back to farming. He needed a nudge to become king and it came from none other than Nahash the eye-gouger.

Nahash and the Ammonites soon rounded up the last 7,000 men of Gad and Rueben who still had both eyes. They had been hiding at Jabesh-Gilead. He made them an offer: Lose an eye and live, or keep your eye and die. They said, "Give us seven days." Then they called for help (1 Samuel 11:3–4).

Word gets back to Saul and he's so furious that he cuts his ox into twelve pieces and uses the bloody oxen parts to issue a strange invitation. He sends a piece to each of the twelve tribes of Israel with this note: *This is what will be done to the oxen of anyone who does not follow Saul and Samuel* (1 Samuel 11:7).

They do, and Saul has an instant army of 330,000 men. He takes them to Jabesh-Gilead and slaughters Nahash and the Ammonites. Israel has its first king and Samuel steps aside as judge, but not without a farewell address. They didn't need a judge if they had a king, but Samuel reminded them: *Only fear the LORD, and serve him faithfully with all your heart* (1 Samuel 12:24).

There is a reference to the "heart" again. Men's hearts will play a major role in the way things unfold. Saul sends most of his army home and keeps only 3,000 men to wipe out a garrison of Philistines, but the Philistines gather a huge army of 30,000 chariots, 6,000 horsemen, and thousands of foot soldiers. Saul calls his troops together and asks Samuel to come out of retirement to offer a sacrifice so they will be successful. But Samuel doesn't come immediately, so Saul does what he sees fit. He offers his own sacrifice. Samuel shows up and says, "What on earth are you doing? You aren't doing what God commanded you. You have a disobedient heart and your kingdom will not continue; the Lord has sought out a man after his own heart." With that, Samuel goes back home.

"DO NOT SPARE THEM"

Nevertheless, Saul routs the Philistines and then takes on the Edomites, the Moabites, and the Ammonites. He is successful wherever he goes. Then God sends Samuel to talk to Saul. He says, *Thus says the Lord of hosts,* "*I will punish the Amalekites for what they did in opposing the Israelites when they came up out of Egypt. Now go and attack Amalek, and utterly destroy all that they have; do not spare them, but kill both man and woman, child and infant, ox and sheep, camel and donkey"* (1 Samuel 15: 2–3).

Saul says, "I can do that." He gathers his army and takes on the Amalekites, but he doesn't kill the sheep and cattle. He takes them as spoils of the war and, on top of that he keeps their king as a prisoner of war.

Word gets to Samuel and he's not pleased. He again confronts Saul with his disobedience:

> *Has the Lord as great delight in burnt offerings and sacrifices,*
> *as in obedience to the voice of the Lord?*
> *Surely, to obey is better than sacrifice,*
> *and to heed than the fat of rams.*
> *For rebellion is no less a sin than divination,*
> *   and stubbornness is like iniquity and idolatry.*
> *Because you have rejected the word of the Lord,*
> *   he has also rejected you from being king.*
> (1 Samuel 15:22–23)

Clearly, Samuel had to find someone else who would be a man after God's own heart.

A NEW KING IS CHOSEN

God sends Samuel to a little town that would become one of the most famous birthplaces in the world. He goes to Bethlehem and visits the house of Jesse. One by one, Jesse presents his sons to

Samuel and each time, Samuel thinks, *This must be the one.* And one by one, God says, "Not this one." And so we learn this pivotal truth from the story of David: *The LORD does not see as mortals see; they look on the outward appearance, but the LORD looks on the heart* (1 Samuel 16:7). What God looks for isn't what impresses us. God doesn't choose leaders like we choose them. God looks on the heart.

After seven sons have passed and God has said no to each, Samuel asks Jesse, "Do you have any others?"

Jesse said, "Yes, but he's young and he's out in the field, tending sheep." Samuel insisted that they bring him in.

> *Now he was ruddy, and had beautiful eyes, and was handsome. The LORD said, "Rise and anoint him; for this is the one." Then Samuel took the horn of oil, and anointed him in the presence of his brothers; and the spirit of the LORD came mightily upon David from that day forward.* (1 Samuel 16:12–13)

It's the beginning of David's story, a wonderful story of the shepherd boy anointed to lead the people of Israel. In this story, we see all of the tension found in today's Middle East conflict between the Jews and their Palestinian neighbors; all that animosity started 3,500 years ago. But there's more.

WHAT DOES GOD SEE IN YOUR HEART?

Again and again, this story confronts us with the fact that God looks at each individual's heart—the purposeful center of our being. So what does God see in your heart? Does God see someone who is obedient, disciplined, and faithful, or someone who "does what he sees fit?" Would God find someone who is caught up in his own wants and desires, or someone who truly has a heart for doing

God's will? Would God see in you the same things that He saw in David's heart?

As we learn more about him, we'll find that David had devotion to God, the courage to lead, genuine love for other human beings, and the strength to obey—devotion, courage, love, and strength—virtues that would make anyone an extraordinary servant of God. David often fell short of being the man God had created him to be; yet God was not through with him, even then.

What does God see in your heart? And what can God do with someone like you? The answers may surprise you.

Discussion Questions

1. While settling the land of Canaan, the Israelites submitted their legal disputes to a group of respected leaders called "judges." Who was the last judge? Why did he feel rejected by his people?

2. Who was chosen as the next leader of the Israelites? How did he show leadership potential?

3. What did the enemy king Nahash order his soldiers to do to the men of Israel? If you were one of his victims, how would you have felt about Nahash? About your own leaders?

4. Write a brief prayer that you might have made to God if you were one of Nahash's victims. How would you describe God in this prayer? How would you describe the old judge who was still your leader? What would you ask God to do in this situation?

5. What did King Saul ask Samuel to do when their army faced overwhelming odds in battle?

6. When Saul took matters into his own hands, what conclusion did Samuel reach? What subsequent actions proved that he was right?

7. Put yourself in the place of Samuel, reviewing Jesse's sons as candidates for king. What qualities would you look for?

8. The Bible says we tend to judge people by their outward appearance, but "the Lord looks on the heart" (1 Samuel 16:7). What do you think that means?

9. What questions might you ask candidates for a place of leadership in your congregation, in order to assess their potential as God does?

For Further Study

1. What did the Philistine "neighbors" do to assure that the Israelites would not be a military threat to them? (1 Samuel 13:19–22.)

2. How did Saul and his men prevail against the Philistines in spite of this disadvantage? (Read 1 Samuel 14:18–23).

3. Read 1 Samuel 15:32–33 to see what old Judge Samuel did with the enemy king that Saul had taken as a prisoner of war. Why was such brutal justice warranted? (Hint: Look at the beginning of the same chapter.)

COURAGE TO FACE GIANTS
1 Samuel 17:31–37, 48–49

David had great courage, which became apparent even when he was a boy. In the previous chapter, we learned about David's selection as the anointed one of Israel. To find a new king for Israel, God sent Samuel to Bethlehem and the house of Jesse. All of Jesse's sons passed before Samuel until they had to call the last one, the young David, to come in from tending sheep. God revealed to Samuel that the shepherd boy would be the new king, so the old priest anointed him. We learned that what God looks for isn't what impresses us. God doesn't choose leaders as we choose them. God looks on the heart. It's the beginning of the wonderful story of God's anointed one, which in Hebrew is a word that our English Bibles transliterate as "the Messiah."

THE BOY AND THE GIANT

We then come to the familiar story of David and Goliath. After their partial defeat and humiliation at the hand of the Israelites in 1 Samuel 14, the Philistines seem eager to regain not only the military dominance they once held over Israel, but their sense of pride as well. The two armies square off approximately fifteen miles southwest of Jerusalem, digging in on opposite sides of the Elah Valley and setting up camp on the sides of two mountains, each of which slopes down to the valley with a brook running between.

For a long time there is a standoff, with loud shouting and all of the hype of war, but with no real contact between the two armies and no casualties. Saul and his army do not really want to fight, and neither do the Philistines, so they just hold their ground. At the beginning of 1 Samuel 17, we are introduced to Goliath as he comes to the front line of the standoff.

> *And there came out from the camp of the Philistines a champion named Goliath, of Gath, whose height was six cubits and a span. He had a helmet of bronze on his head, and he was armed with a coat of mail; the weight of the coat was five thousand shekels of bronze. He had greaves of bronze on his legs and a javelin of bronze slung between his shoulders.* (1 Samuel 17:4–6)

You get the idea. Goliath is a big man, "six cubits and a span," or nearly ten feet tall. He is well-protected and well-armed, carrying both a javelin and a sword. Verse 24 says, *All the Israelites, when they saw the man, fled from him and were very much afraid.* Goliath came forward to offer a deal to the Israelites. Instead of the two armies fighting, he suggested, they could choose a man from the ranks of the Israelites to challenge Goliath one-on-one. Whoever won the matchup would win the war. Goliath would come forward twice a day, morning and evening, for forty days to see if anyone was ready to take him up on his offer.

While all of this was taking place, David was still back home, tending the family's sheep. David's three oldest brothers—Eliab, Abinadab, and Shammah—were a part of the Israelite army. Their father, Jesse, was concerned about his three sons on the front line, so he gave a task to young David: He would go and check on the welfare of his brothers and take supplies to them. David did as his father asked and went off to find the army. He left their supplies in charge of the army's quartermaster; then went to the frontline to greet his brothers and check on them.

> *As he talked with them, the champion, the Philistine of Gath, Goliath by name, came up out of the ranks of the Philistines, and spoke the same words as before. And David heard him.*
> (1 Samuel 17:23)

David was interested in Goliath's proposal, so he asked about it around the Israelite army camp. His questions aroused the anger of his oldest brother, Eliab, who thought David had simply come to watch the battle. Eliab's words were pointed and demeaning:

> *"Why have you come down? With whom have you left those few sheep in the wilderness? I know your presumption and the evil of your heart; for you have come down just to see the battle."* David said, *"What have I done now? It was only a question."*
> (1 Samuel 17:28–29)

We don't know David's decision-making process but he decided right then and there that he would take on Goliath. He went before King Saul and volunteered to go one-on-one with the giant. Saul took some convincing, and a large section of the seventeenth chapter is devoted to David's reciting his qualifications to Saul. He said, "I've struck down lions and bears that were stealing sheep. Their paws were no match for me—God is on my side. I can do this." Finally, Saul relented and said to David, *"Go, and may the Lord be with you!"* (1 Samuel 17:37)

Saul outfits him with a soldier's armor and a bronze helmet. I have this picture of a little kid in oversized armor that weighs more than he does, becoming nearly immobilized by the bulk and the weight. He tries to walk but can't. After stumbling around, it's clear that wearing the armor is not a good idea, so he gives it back to Saul. He takes back his much more familiar shepherd's staff and bag, as well as his sling.

A SHEPHERD'S WEAPONS

In the children's telling of this story, we most often think of this sling as a slingshot like the ones some of us had as children. (Mine was taken away when I was ten, after I put a stone through a neighbor's window.) However, David's sling would have been different. He would have operated it by spinning it off to one side and letting the stone fly at just the precise moment to hit its intended target. Ballistic experts believe this kind of sling in the hands of an experienced slinger (that's what they were called) would have matched the power of a modern handgun.

David selects five smooth stones from the creek and sets off to encounter Goliath. First Samuel 17:41–47 recounts the conversation between David and Goliath when they come within shouting distance of one another. And shout they do. It reminds us of two boys in a schoolyard trying to intimidate one another with words and threats. They curse one another, threaten to beat each other, and feed their adversary's remains to the birds and the animals. David says that Goliath has a sword and javelin, but he has God, whom Goliath has defied (v 47). However, the actual battle between David and Goliath takes only two verses of scripture:

> *When the Philistine drew nearer to meet David, David ran quickly toward the battle line to meet the Philistine. David put his hand in his bag, took out a stone, slung it, and struck the Philistine on his forehead; the stone sank into his forehead, and he fell face down on the ground.* (1 Samuel 17:48–49)

That's where most children's stories end, but the gory conclusion takes this from a PG-13 to an R-rated film. If you think you can handle this, read verse 51:

> *Then David ran and stood over the Philistine; he grasped his sword, drew it out of its sheath, and killed him; then he cut off his head with it.* (1 Samuel 17:51)

With Goliath out of the way, the story ends with the Israelite army's being emboldened and chasing the Philistines back to their own land. When Saul asks who this "stripling" is, General Abner brings David before the king with Goliath's bloody head in his hand (vv 55–58).

YOUR GIANTS AND MINE

Lots of questions could be addressed in this great story, but let me ask two: Who are the giants we face today, and what gives us the courage to face them?

We all have giants in our lives. I'm not talking about ridiculously tall Uncle Ted, but the giants that derail our lives from being all they can be. Our giants are different. What you perceive as a giant may be nothing to me, and what I perceive as a giant you may have already conquered. Such giants are often in our minds rather than in the visible, physical world, but this doesn't mean they are any less real.

Our giants carry names like fear, hopelessness, bitterness, guilt, shame, loneliness, and worry. These giants stand in the way of our fully following God. The good news is that our giants are vulnerable.

We are entranced by David and Goliath stories. That's why we love the movie "Hoosiers," which tells how Milan beats Muncie Central to win the 1954 Indiana state basketball championship. (For as much attention as that game received, perhaps more striking was a semistate game two games before that, when Milan beat Crispus Attucks, led by high school sophomore Oscar Robertson.)

While sports metaphors nicely illustrate the courage of the underdog, there are examples in all facets of life. The civil rights movement of the 1950s and 1960s was full of people who had the courage of David, people who refused to be intimidated by giants in their way. There are stories of heroes on the battlefield and in the corporate boardroom, who see giant problems as obstacles but not roadblocks to the future.

Best-selling author Malcolm Gladwell recently published a book titled, *David & Goliath: Underdogs, Misfits and the Art of Battling Giants*. In it he proposes that giants are seldom as invincible as they seem. He cites a number of scientific studies that suggest Goliath's size could have been attributed to a birth defect that gave him poor peripheral vision, which allowed David to circle him without being seen.[1]

In other words, this giant who paralyzed an entire army regiment for over a month had a vulnerability that allowed him to be beaten, but those who saw him (save David) only saw a giant. Ultimately, the point of Gladwell's book is that problems are rarely as daunting as they seem on the surface. Powerful adversaries are not as powerful as they seem; they have weaknesses. By the same token, the weak are not as weak as they seem; they have power in undiscovered places.

Being an underdog can change people in ways that we often fail to appreciate. The courage of an underdog can open doors, create opportunities, educate and enlighten, and otherwise make possible what may have seemed unthinkable.[2]

Goliath was covered in heavy bronze, making it difficult to move, because he was prepared for battle at close range. He realized too late that David had changed the rules of battle. David was agile, able to run at this giant and aim his stone projectile with stunning precision. He used his experience to attack Goliath at a point of weakness.

GOING WITH GOD

Moreover, David attacked Goliath *in the name of the L*ORD *of hosts* (v 45). Gladwell's writings, while revolutionary to some, square with the teachings of Mrs. Moore, my elementary Sunday school teacher. She said that David's courage came from the fact that he knew God was with him.

King Saul, like Goliath, thought of power only in terms of physical might. Neither appreciated the fact that power can come in other forms as well, such as breaking conventional wisdom or substituting brainpower for physical strength.

As I read the familiar story of David and Goliath, I want what David had—not smooth stones or a bag to carry them in, but the courage to see the giants in my life more clearly, to see them as obstacles that I can get over and work around. I want the wisdom to see them in this perspective when I move—no, run—toward them with God on my side.

This story demonstrates not so much that David was great, but that the God he served, the God Who went before him, was greater than his adversary. By contrast, King Saul seemed to focus on the size of the enemy rather than on the size of God.

We all have giants that seem much greater than we, and we can't imagine they are the least bit vulnerable. But by trusting in God and not in ourselves, by giving Him the glory rather than taking the credit ourselves, by looking for new and creative ways to be more agile than the giants we face, we can render the giants powerless to disrupt our lives.

Discussion Questions

1. What did we learn about the Philistines in the previous chapter? What do you think caused their ongoing conflict with the Israelites?

2. Why did David's brothers think he came to the battlefield? Might Samuel's anointing of David have caused his brothers to resent him? Why else might they have wanted David to go home?

3. The armor that King Saul gave David was a liability instead of an asset. How is this similar to our own efforts to defend ourselves from the giants of life?

4. List some "giants" that would prevent you from following God. Which of them pose the greatest threats to you today?

5. Instead of hiding from Goliath, David confronted him directly. Describe some ways you might confront the giants that are most threatening to you.

6. If the stone killed Goliath, why did David cut off his head? How might you do this to a giant that threatens you after you have defeated it?

7. When we hide from something we fear or try to ignore it, does the threat usually subside? How might our cowering make our giants stronger?

8. Recall a time when a problem that you feared failed to materialize. How did you feel about that? What did you learn from that experience?

9. What practices make your courage stronger? Weaker?

10. List spiritual weapons you can use to combat "giants" that threaten you now. How can you gain skill in using each of these weapons?

For Further Study

1. Compare David's relationship with his brothers to that between Joseph and his brothers (Genesis 37:3–11). What similarities do you see? What values can the youngest, smallest sibling of a family learn from these stories?

2. The fight between David and Goliath—called a "trial by combat"—was fairly common in the ancient world. Do some research on this term. What did armies believe such a one-on-one contest revealed?

FAITHFUL LOVE
1 Samuel 20:12-17

The moment Goliath fell to the ground, everything about David's life changed. "Being an underdog can change people in ways that we often fail to appreciate: it can open doors and create opportunities and educate and enlighten and make possible what might otherwise have seemed unthinkable."[3] The doors that opened for David were fame and celebrity, fear and disgrace. When he woke up that day, he had no idea of the way his life was about to change with the sling of a rock. If David could have known how his life was about to change, it might have given him pause.

David's newfound notoriety meant leaving behind his family and his sheep, moving to the palace where he would play his harp for Saul, and being made head over the army even though he was not yet twenty years old. It meant walking through the streets of the towns of Israel leading back to Jerusalem with women singing,

> "Saul has killed his thousands, and David his ten thousands."
>
> Saul was very angry, for this saying displeased him. He said, "They have ascribed to David ten thousands, and to me they have ascribed thousands; what more can he have but the kingdom?" So Saul eyed David from that day on. (1 Samuel 18:7–9)

So did another, Jonathan, King Saul's son. This incident began a deep bond of love and friendship that is the third chapter of David's story. It would not be an exaggeration to say that Jonathan and David were closer than blood brothers. It would also not be an exaggeration to suggest that God must have blessed their friendship, because no two people could have been less alike.

David was the seventh son of Jesse, a poor shepherd family. He grew up living off the land and surviving on leftovers. His skin was described as "ruddy" and his hands calloused from holding a shepherd's crook, tending sheep. As the seventh son, he stood to inherit absolutely nothing when his father died.

On the other hand, Jonathan was the prince of Israel and as such would have grown up in the lap of luxury in the royal city of Jerusalem. He was the king's firstborn son and heir to the throne. More than likely his skin was pale and his hands soft. We'd say he was "born with a silver spoon in his mouth"—a crown on his head. I'm sure from the earliest moment of his consciousness Jonathan was told he would one day be king, that he would inherit it all.

To say that these two young men were mismatched is an understatement, and yet they represent the deepest friendship described in the Bible. *The soul of Jonathan was bound to the soul of David, and Jonathan loved him as his own soul* (1 Samuel 18:1). This was more than the love a youth may have for a war hero. *Jonathan made a covenant with David, because he loved him as his own soul* (1 Samuel 18:3). He took off his robe and gave it to David. He handed him his armor and sword. He gave David the symbols of his pending kingship to demonstrate the depth of this covenantal love.

Think about this happening today. Prince Charles will eventually become King of England. Imagine the ever-attractive and popular

Prince William, heir apparent to his father's throne, stripping himself of his gold and crimson sash, handing over his sword, and symbolically giving his throne to a shepherd from Scotland. Can you imagine the stir it would cause? What a nasty look Kate might give him, considering the implication for cute little Prince George! If this pledge of covenantal love were to take place, don't you think Charles would keep his eye on William's shepherd buddy from that day forward?

ROYAL TREACHERY

Saul keeps more than an eye on David. He begins trying to kill David the very next day. David is playing the harp in the royal palace when King Saul throws his spear at him, trying to pin David against the wall. That doesn't work so he sends David into battle, making him the head of the army although he is young and has only one combat experience to his credit, the slingshot victory over Goliath. David has no leadership experience, yet God is with him. David is very successful in battle. He is soon loved not only by Jonathan but by all of Israel and Judah.

Saul tries another scheme. He offers to give David his daughter's hand in marriage if he will personally kill 100 Philistines, circumcise their corpses, and bring back the trophies of their emasculation as a sign of loyalty to Saul. Saul is convinced that David will be killed. Instead, he is successful again and Saul has to hand over his daughter. Everything Saul tries, fails.

Finally, Saul takes his son Jonathan and a group of servants into confidence, sharing with them that he wants to kill David. But because Jonathan loves David, he convinces his father not to kill him. Jonathan personally brings David back into the palace.

This accommodation is short-lived. A few days later, while David is again playing the harp, Saul becomes enraged and throws a spear at him. David flees, terrified, to his wife, thinking because she is family he'll be safe, but Michal knows better. She lowers David on a rope through the window so he can run away. Then, *Michal took an idol and laid it on the bed; she put a net of goats' hair on its head, and covered it with the clothes* (1 Samuel 19:13). She tells the guards who come to get him that David is sick in bed. They fall for it, which buys him a little time. But then Saul shows up, the ruse is discovered, and he is furious with his daughter.

A PRINCE'S INTERVENTION

Meanwhile, Jonathan finds David hiding in fear in Ramah. He offers to intercede once again with his father, to convince Saul there is no reason to kill David. Jonathan says to David,

> *"If I am still alive, show me the faithful love of the LORD; but if I die, never cut off your faithful love from my house...." Thus Jonathan made a covenant with the house of David...Jonathan made David swear again by his love for him; for he loved him as he loved his own life.* (1 Samuel 20:14–17)

It is wonderful, incredible love in the face of great tragedy. I wish I could tell you there is a happy ending to this episode, but there is not.

Jonathan tries to convince his father to make peace with David, but instead Saul turns his rage and anger toward Jonathan, accusing him of treason. This time he throws a spear at his own son. Once again, he misses. (Clearly, King Saul would never represent Israel in a javelin contest. His aim was horrible.)

Jonathan and David meet and weep together about a friendship that was sacred but fettered by the hatred of Jonathan's father. They part, only to meet one last time before Jonathan's death on the battlefield. Jonathan meets David at Horesh and reminds him of God's promise to make David king. He literally *strengthened his hand through the LORD.... Then the two of them made a covenant before the LORD* (1 Samuel 23:16, 18).

This is an example of radical, risking-taking, death-defying friendship based on faithful love. It was, as the Song of Solomon describes it, love as *strong as death* (Song 8:6). For Jonathan and David, no amount of personal danger could damage the brotherly love they had for each other.

EVER-FAITHFUL LOVE

In Hebrew, there is a special name for this type of love: *Hesed*. Throughout this story, the word *hesed* is translated, "faithful love." It is covenantal, binding one person to another. Remember Jonathan's request, "Show me the faithful love of the LORD" (1 Samuel 20:14). Insert the Hebrew and it would be, "Show me the *hesed* of the LORD." Show me God-like, covenantal love. So *Jonathan made a covenant with David, because he loved him as his own soul* (1 Samuel 18:3). These men demonstrated to each other the same kind of faithful love that God had shown toward them.

Hesed is to love as God loves. It is risky love because it persists beyond any sin, betrayal, or brokenness, and it graciously extends forgiveness.

> *For the Lord will not reject forever. Although he causes grief, he will have compassion according to the abundance*

of his steadfast love [hesed]; for he does not willingly afflict or grieve anyone. (Lamentations 3:31–33)

Hesed connotes not just a feeling, but also an action. It is love that intervenes on behalf of loved ones and comes to their rescue. *Hesed* is often translated as "mercy," "loving-kindness," or "faithful love," but none of these words fully conveys the fact that *hesed* acts out of unwavering love, even in the most daunting of circumstances.

David and Jonathan demonstrated this extraordinary love—a love that knows no fear, love that is strong as death. Only one friendship, one love goes deeper and further in its radical risk-taking. It is the love offered us by another shepherd from Bethlehem—Jesus.

LOVING LIKE JESUS

The Gospels describe many times when Jesus offers the same covenantal love, but none is more powerful than His pledge of love in the Upper Room. Do you remember? *"No one has greater love than this, to lay down one's life for one's friends"* (John 15:13). Then He adds, *"You are my friends"* (John 15:14). He is speaking not only to the Twelve who dined with Him that night, but also to you as you read His promise. If you know Jesus, then you have a Friend who has pledged His love, His *hesed*, to you personally. This love can't be thwarted, not even by death.

This kind of love is contagious. It has to be shared. So Jesus says, *"This is my commandment, that you love one another as I have loved you"* (John 15:12). If we receive Jesus' love, we are to give it away; we are to love like Jesus Himself. Long before Jesus made that challenge to us, Jonathan and David lived it. They demonstrated the undying, covenantal love of *hesed* and challenged us to extend it to others.

Yes, David's story is about his heart. He had a heart for God, a heart filled with courage and love. Do you love others as David did? As Jonathan did? As Jesus did? How might your life look different if you did?

You may have your doubts about how to answer that. Don't worry. We will see in the next chapter that even David, who demonstrated this covenantal love, had doubts about his ability to remain faithful in his love.

Discussion Questions

1. About how old do you think David and Jonathan were when they formed this bond of friendship? Some believe that young men are more likely to commit themselves to this kind of relationship, since they have few other loyalties. Do you agree?

2. Did you ever have a "bosom buddy" like this? What were the circumstances when you formed this friendship? Are you still close to this person? If not, what changed?

3. How is *hesed* different from romantic love? Different from hero worship?

4. "I've got your back" is a recent expression of the kind of commitment David and Jonathan made to one another. What do you visualize when you hear that phrase?

5. Why did David and Jonathan's commitment to one another arouse such anger in King Saul?

6. What evidence does the Bible give that both David and Jonathan remained loyal to King Saul?

7. How might a congregation of Christians show this kind of "steadfast love" for their local community? For the global community?

8. Eugene H. Peterson says, "We can *act* ourselves into a new way of feeling much quicker than we can *feel* ourselves into a new way of acting."[4] Apply this principle to *hesed*. If you don't feel this kind of love for others, how can you change?

For Further Study

1. Based on what you already know of the history of Israel, identify some times when God continued to show His love for these people despite their unfaithfulness to Him.

2. Some Christians cite Matthew 5:33–35 and James 5:12 as proof that they should not make a pledge to do something; however, *hesed* involves a mutual pledge between two persons. It is "faithful love" because they remain faithful to their pledge. How do you reconcile these teachings of Scripture? What specifically do you believe the Matthew 5 and James 5 texts warn against?

DOUBTING AND TRUSTING GOD
1 Samuel 21; 22:1

Do you ever doubt God? That's a silly question; of course you do. You can't be human without experiencing doubt. Doubts can come during a lengthy illness, when plans fade, when tragedy occurs. Wayward children, marriage difficulties, loss of job, financial challenges, struggling parents—all can bring on doubt.

I wonder how people want me to answer when I get asked, "Randy, do you ever doubt?" Perhaps they want me to say *no* because they want their pastor to have a rock-solid faith. But when I answer *yes*, perhaps they say, "Whew! That's good to hear. I'm glad I'm not the only one."

Everyone doubts. Even those closest to Jesus doubted. In the last scene of Jesus' time on earth, Matthew says, *When they saw him, they worshiped him; but some doubted* (Matthew 28:17). If those who walked with Jesus doubted, then you and I can expect to have moments when we struggle to believe, times when we might ask like David, *How long, O LORD? Will you forget me forever? How long will you hide your face from me?* (Psalm 13:1)

That's not where David was when we began his story. He must have felt great joy and anticipation when Samuel anointed him to be the next king of Israel. In subsequent events, David proved to have a heart of courage and faithfulness. We saw in the previous chapter that a special love forms between David and the king's son Jonathan, as the king's plot to kill David unfolds. They swear a covenant of *faithful love of the LORD* (1 Samuel 20:14). "Faithful love" is our English translation of the Hebrew word *hesed*. It denotes a radical, risk-taking, strong-as-death love, such as we see between Jonathan and David. Based on this risk-taking, death-defying love, Jonathan tries to intercede with his father, King Saul, to deter him from killing David. He fails and now David is on the run. He runs straight into doubt.

This is a sad chapter in David's story, not because David experiences doubt. As we said, doubt is inevitable. Rather, it is sad because David misses all of the places where God tries to remind him how to handle his doubt.

DOUBT AT EVERY TURN

David first runs to a community of priests in the city of Nob, which was outside of Jerusalem near the Mount of Olives. Because the Temple had yet to be built, Nob serves as the sacred place of the Tabernacle. When David shows up, the high priest *Ahimelech came trembling to meet David, and said to him, "Why are you alone, and no one with you?"* (1 Samuel 21:1). Now that's a fair question. Ahimelech knows that David is head over all of the armies of Israel and God has anointed him the next king. So why does he show up here alone?

My wife and I were once on a trolley tour of Washington, D.C., when we saw a motorcade traveling with sirens. It was comprised of half a dozen motorcycle police and four or five black SUVs in front of a couple of limousines. Our tour guide said, "Let's see if that's the president. If it is, there will be paramedics at the end of the motorcade." There weren't, so he said, "Maybe it's the vice-president or a foreign head of state."

David's in that class now. Because he is head of the army and anointed the next king, he should be traveling with security, but he shows up alone. Ahimelech immediately knows something strange is going on, so he asks David why he's traveling by himself. David replies, *The king has charged me with a matter, and said to me, "No one must know anything of the matter about which I send you...."* (1 Samuel 21:2). That's a lie. David is not on a secret assignment from Saul; he's running from Saul. But then he adds another lie: *"I have made an appointment with the young men for such and such a place"* (1 Samuel 21:2). There are no men waiting for him. When you give into doubt, it can run you right off the moral high ground. Lost in his doubt about God, David lies, and the lies keep coming.

"Uh, Ahimelech, I need some food. Can you give me five loaves of bread?" Now think about this again. What head of state travels with no provisions? Ahimelech is just shaking his head. *"I have no ordinary bread at hand,"* he says apologetically, *"only holy bread"* (1 Samuel 21:4).

David should have known this. The holy bread was called the *Presence* or sometimes the *Showbread* because it was offered to God in the Tabernacle worship services. Leviticus 25 instructs the priests to place twelve loaves of bread in the Tabernacle each Sabbath. This consecrated bread was to be replaced a week later, on the following Sabbath. It was a gift to God to honor Him for His faithfulness. Whatever bread God didn't eat, whatever bread was left over from the previous week, became food for the priests. It represented the manna that God provided Israel as they wandered the wilderness for forty years.

This is highly significant. Remember that as the Israelites wandered, they worried. Doubt raised its ugly head and they said, "How are we going to eat? We'll starve out here." They didn't trust that God would provide. So God rained down manna, which they collected each morning, and then they knew they could trust God (Exodus 16).

Ahimelech says he only has the holy bread and it is reserved for the priests. But he wonders aloud if he might share some of it with David and his men, *provided that the young men have kept themselves from women* (1 Samuel 21:4). Ahimelech is considering an exception. No one but priests were supposed to eat the bread of *Presence*, but Ahimelech is willing to give it to David's band as long as they are ritualistically pure according to the Holiness Code.

Having lied to the priest several times, what's one more? So David tells a whopper: *"Indeed women have been kept from us as always when I go on an expedition…the young men are holy even when it is a common journey"* (1 Samuel 21:5). Do you hear what he is saying? "My soldiers are celibate; clean as a whistle. They never fraternize with women." Right!

THE DOUBTER'S ART OF SELF-DEFENSE

Ahimelech hands over five loaves of the *Presence*, the sacred showbread that represents the gift of manna in the wilderness, an icon of God's trustworthiness. Right then and there, as David is holding that icon, he should have been reminded to trust in God, but he's so blinded by his doubt he can't see it. He takes the bread and then asks for something more. *"Is there no spear or sword here with you? I did not bring my sword or my weapons with me, because the king's business required haste"* (1 Samuel 21:8). Ahimelech has got be shaking his head again. A general of an army without a weapon? But the priest dutifully says, *"The sword of Goliath the Philistine, whom you killed in the valley of Elah, is here...take it, for there is none here except that one"* (1 Samuel 21:9).

David takes heart. *"There is none like it,"* he says, *"give it to me"* (1 Samuel 21:9).

Goliath's sword is another icon of God's faithfulness, a reminder of God's victory over the Philistines. David the underdog had trusted that God was with him. With one sling of a stone, he felled Goliath and then used the giant's own sword to finish him off. David must have dragged the sword all the way back to Jerusalem, where they put it in the Tabernacle as a reminder to trust in God. If anything should have reminded David to trust God, to put his doubts aside, it should have been that sword. But his heart was still filled with fear and doubt.

David takes the bread of the *Presence* and the sword of Goliath and travels to King Achish of Gath. Does Gath sound familiar? Flip back and you will find that one of the characters in chapter two is described this way: *from the camp of the Philistines a champion named Goliath, of Gath* (1 Samuel 17:4). David has gone over to the Philistines. He has run to the enemy to seek asylum. What is he thinking? Even the servants of Achish think it is weird. They say,

> *"Is this not David the king of the land? Did they not sing to one another of him in dances,*
> *'Saul has killed his thousands,*
>   *and David his ten thousands'?"* (1 Samuel 21:11)

Yes, they did. When David was returning from battle, during his hero's parade, the exultant women sang it over and over. It was an iconic moment in David's young life. For the third time, David has a reminder to trust in God and for a third time, rather than use the past to steel him for the future, he gives into doubt and becomes afraid. Hearing these questions about his true motives for being in Gath, he fears that King Achish and the Philistines will kill him, so he starts acting like a madman, scratching at the city gate like an animal and drooling, his beard covered with spit. It works. The king thinks he's crazy and he has enough crazies around Gath already, so he wants David out of there. By this time, David wants out too. *David left there and escaped to the cave of Adullam* (1 Samuel 22:1). It is in the cave that David comes to his senses and deals with his doubt.

FROM DOUBT TO RENEWED FAITH

We don't know what happened in the cave, but I can imagine him sitting there with the Holy Bread in one hand and the sword of Goliath in the other. Bouncing around in his head is the phrase that the women sang, *"Saul has killed his thousands, and David his ten thousands."* He has three powerful reminders of God's faithfulness. In that moment, something changes and David begins to sing. We know what the lyrics were:

> *People trample on me; all day long foes oppress me;*
> *my enemies trample on me all day long, for many fight against me*
> (Psalm 56:1–2).

Then, maybe holding onto the icons just a bit tighter, he sings,

> *O Most High, when I am afraid, I put my trust in you* (v 3).

He goes on to name his doubt and claim the situation he is in:

They stir up strife, they lurk, they watch my steps.
As they hoped to have my life. (v 6)

But this time, he sings,

This I know, that God is for me. In God, whose word I praise,
   in the LORD, whose word I praise,
in God I trust; I am not afraid.
   What can a mere mortal do to me? (vv 9–11)

How does he know this? Holding the icons, he remembers what God has done for him:

For you have delivered my soul from death, and my feet
from falling, so that I may walk before God in the light of life.
(v 13)

Of course God did. Time and time again, God had delivered him. The icons remind him of God's faithfulness, God's trustworthiness, so praise to God becomes David's refrain. Notice how he repeats it:

I lie down among lions that greedily devour human prey;
their teeth are spears and arrows, their tongues sharp swords.

Be exalted, O God, above the heavens.
   Let your glory be over all the earth. (Psalm 57:4–5)

They set a net for my steps; my soul was bowed down.
They dug a pit in my path, but they have fallen into it
themselves. ...

> *Be exalted, O God, above the heavens.*
> *Let your glory be over all the earth.* (Psalm 57:6, 11)

Psalms 56 and 57 are a record, not just of David's doubt, but also of what he did to manage his doubt. This can be very instructive for us.

This episode comes to an end with David's family coming to him in the cave, and 400 others soon join them. All of them have struggled under King Saul's oppressive rule. David takes command of them. He now has "his men," a small army.

REMINDERS OF GOD'S FAITHFULNESS

I want to close this chapter with a question about your reminders of God's faithfulness: *What are your icons of faith?* What are the "God moments" that you can recall in times of doubt?

Each of us has an icon of faith somewhere in our lives. Maybe it's your parents who nurtured and blessed you as a child. Maybe it is the memory of someone who rescued you in a really difficult time. Maybe it's a hospital bracelet, reminding you of God's healing power. Maybe it's the memory of a dark moment when you thought you wouldn't survive—but you did. Maybe it's a cross, which reminds you that someone led you to Christ, and through Him you are saved.

Everyone has such icons of God's faithfulness. Don't ignore them. David learned this the hard way, and we can learn from him. When in doubt, hold onto your icons of God's faithfulness and keep saying what David said: *This I know, that God is for me* (Psalm 56:9).

The critical thing is not whether we doubt God—we will! The critical thing is how we manage our doubt.

Discussion Questions

1. Are you surprised to see how often David lied to others, even to the priest of the Tabernacle? How do you suppose he justified this in his own mind?

2. David hoped that his Philistine enemies would shelter him from King Saul's wrath. What does this reveal about David's faith?

3. David's experience proves that even a shrewd man can blunder into danger. How does doubting God make us more vulnerable to such mistakes?

4. Which of God's promises are you most likely to doubt?

5. When you doubt God, do you try to take care of your problems by yourself? Some call this "bootstrap Christianity," because we try to pull ourselves up by our own bootstraps. Why doesn't this work?

6. If we dwell on cherishing memories of God's past faithfulness that can become an empty kind of sentimentalism. How do we avoid that? How do we make sure our memories build our faith in God, rather than simply longing for the past?

7. *"This I know, that God is for me"* (Psalm 56:9). Apply this affirmation of faith to an obstacle you are facing. How does it look now?

For Further Study

1. Read each of the following scriptures and answer the question, What happened to these people who allowed doubt to control their lives?

    - Matthew 13:54–58
    - Romans 11:19–21
    - Hebrews 3:14–19

2. Read about the father of a demon-possessed boy (Mark 9:14–24). What do you think he meant when he said he "believed" Jesus, but still had "unbelief"? Did his unbelief prevent Jesus from healing his son?

MERCY VS. REVENGE
1 Samuel 26:21–25

King Saul is worried that David is a threat to his kingship and there is conflict. He tries to kill him, first by throwing spears at him and then by sending him on dangerous assignments. So David runs for his life and begins to doubt God.

Doubt can blind you and cause you to fail morally, and it does both for David. He lies to the high priest about his circumstances but receives three important reminders of God's trustworthiness. David is so blinded by his fear that he fails to see the significance of them. Eventually, he finds himself in a cave, mulling over these icons of faith—bread that represents the manna God provided in the wilderness, Goliath's sword, and the women's song after David killed the giant. There in the gloom, David begins to sing, *This I know, that God is for me* (Psalm 56:9). His trust renewed, he is soon joined by his family and a small army.

Yet Saul continues trying to kill David. *Saul sought him [David] every day, but the LORD did not give him into his hand* (1 Samuel 23:14). David and his army, now 600 strong, are in the wilderness of En Gedi. This is an oasis rimmed by limestone cliffs above the Dead Sea. There are hundreds of caves here, which made it a perfect place to hide. But no hiding place is safe if informers reveal your location.

When spies tell Saul where David is, he gathers an army of 3,000 and heads to En Gedi to kill David.

TARGET OF OPPORTUNITY

Traveling with an army in a wilderness means "roughing it," even in the best of circumstances, so when Saul and the army arrive in En Gedi, Saul chooses a cave to answer the call of nature. As luck would have it, it is the very cave where David and his men are hiding. What an opportunity! Saul has been delivered into David's hand. He's vulnerable and alone, clueless that danger is behind him. In the darkness of the cave, David can easily kill him.

"Don't get mad, David, get even!" That's what we'd say and, sure enough, plenty of voices offer that opinion. His men whisper, "This is God's day. God has delivered your enemy to you. Take this dagger and kill him." So David sneaks up on Saul and takes out his knife. But instead of killing him, David quietly *cut off a corner of Saul's cloak* (1 Samuel 24:4). David then slips away and returns to his men. They are outraged that David didn't kill Saul, but David rebukes them and prevents them from taking matters into their own hands.

As Saul leaves the cave, David calls out to him. Saul turns around, and David falls to the ground in obeisance. He asks:

> "Why do you listen to the words of those who say, 'David seeks to do you harm'? This very day your eyes have seen how the LORD gave you into my hand in the cave; and some urged me to kill you, but I spared you. I said, 'I will not raise my hand against my lord; for he is the LORD's anointed.'" (1 Samuel 24:9–10)

It is hard to imagine what went through Saul's mind at that moment—embarrassment perhaps, for being seen in such a compromised position. Perhaps he felt fear, realizing that indeed he could have been killed. Under similar circumstances, some people would laugh and congratulate themselves that they had dodged a bullet. Others would cry with relief, and that is what Saul does. *"You are more righteous than I,"* he cries, *"for you have repaid me good, whereas I have repaid you evil"* (1 Samuel 24:17). Saul would not have spared an adversary like this; he would have shown no mercy. But David had a heart of mercy. Mercy is grace shown to someone you have the power to punish or harm. David extends that grace to Saul. In an instant, he could have dispatched Saul with his sword. But David respected the one whom God had anointed king and trusted the timing of Saul's defeat to God.

Saul appears repentant. He says to David, *"So may the Lord reward you with good for what you have done to me this day. Now I know that you shall surely be king, and that the kingdom of Israel shall be established in your hand"* (1 Samuel 24:19–20). Then he walks away. Though Saul's words seem contrite, David knows better. He withdraws with his men to his stronghold.

ANOTHER OPPORTUNITY

There is a brief interlude in which David gets married to a Carmel housewife. (In 1 Samuel 25, David meets Abigail, the wife of Nabal. Abigail and Nabal own a large number of sheep and goats in Carmel. When Nabal has a heart attack and dies, David and Abigail marry.) But there is no time for a honeymoon because Saul renews his pursuit of David.

The Ziphites tell Saul that David is hiding in the hills of Hachilah. Saul gathers his army and determines that he will not make the same mistake as the last time. He encamps opposite Hachilah in the

Jeshimon desert and surrounds himself with his army. When night falls, David and one of his men, Abishai, sneak into Saul's camp to spy on the situation. Surprisingly, they find themselves in the middle of the camp without being challenged. They step over the general of the army, Abner, who is serving as the bodyguard of King Saul. Both Abner and Saul are out cold. At the king's head are a water jug and a spear. Abishai is beyond excited. He whispers to David, *"God has given your enemy into your hand today; now therefore let me pin him to the ground with one stroke of the spear; I will not strike him twice"* (1 Samuel 26:8).

You can understand Abishai's feelings. Saul is relentless in his pursuit to kill them. What would you do? After all of the months and years of running and hiding, both Abishai and David must have been tempted to put it to an end.

But David again refuses. *David said to Abishai, "Do not destroy him; for who can raise his hand against the LORD's anointed, and be guiltless?"* (1 Samuel 26:9). Instead, David and Abishai take Saul's spear and water jug and sneak back out of the camp. The next morning, we again see David's heart of mercy in a scene that is also tinged with a little bit of comedy.

As the sun rises, David stands on the hill of Hachilah and shouts down into the valley for General Abner. The hills have a megaphone effect, so everyone in the valley can hear him. "Abner!" he shouts.

"Who are you that calls to the king?" Abner replies (v 14). He doesn't recognize David's voice and David isn't about to tell him.

"Why then have you not kept watch over your lord the king? For one of the people came in to destroy your lord the king. This thing that you have done is not good. As the LORD lives, you deserve to die, because you have not kept watch over your lord, the LORD's

anointed. See now, where is the king's spear, or the water jar that was at his head?" (vv 15–16).

I imagine Saul pushing Abner out of the way to shout back, "David, is that you?" He knows good and well it is David. He recognizes that voice. It is the one who used to play the harp and sing to him. It is the voice of the one who gave him back a piece of his cloak. He knows who has been merciful to him before and has once again shown amazing mercy.

David shouts, "Why are you doing this? God doesn't want this. I'm not going to raise my hand against you because you are God's anointed. Here's your spear back. I spared your life, now spare mine. Show mercy."

Then Saul said, "I have done wrong; come back, my son David, for I will never harm you again, because my life was precious in your sight today; I have been a fool, and have made a great mistake." (v 21)

Given Saul's easy tendency to say, "Sorry," is there any reason for David to believe that he truly means what he's saying now? Of course not. David is hopeful but not foolish. He simply responds, "Just as I considered your life valuable today, I hope you'll do the same."

Then Saul said to David, "Blessed be you, my son David! You will do many things and will succeed in them." So David went his way, and Saul returned to his place. (v 25)

So they part, never to see each other again. Saul continues to pursue David and David takes refuge among their erstwhile enemies, the Philistines.

TWO WAYS TO DEAL WITH ADVERSARIES

As this episode comes to an end, we see two contrasting ways of dealing with adversaries. Saul pursued and tried to deceive his rival, when in fact he meant to kill him. David consistently showed mercy and an unwillingness to harm his enemy. Consumed with jealousy, Saul sought revenge with his own hands. Because of his faith in God, David waited for God to work things out according to His own timing, even when opportunities arose for David to avenge the wrongs that had been done to him. Saul's heart was hardened, filled with anger and rage; David's was filled with mercy and grace.

In the interest of happy endings, we might wish this were a story of repentance and forgiveness. Sadly, it isn't. It is a story about a man offering mercy to an adversary who never changed.

Which of these two men are you like? What's in your heart, mercy or revenge? We all have *Sauls* in our lives—people who hurt us and show no signs of sorrow, people who wrong us and show no signs of real repentance. Perhaps someone in your past has terribly abused and mistreated you. Perhaps you have a *Saul* in your business life, a dishonest and predatory person who pursues you night and day. Perhaps there's a family member who won't let go of an issue or conflict between you. When you have a *Saul* in your life, it is very hard to respond with grace and forbearance.

David shows us the way. Because he has a heart for God, he acts with courage, love, faithfulness, and mercy. When we show mercy to our adversaries, we reflect the character of God Himself. This is why Jesus said, *"Blessed are the merciful, for they will receive mercy"* (Matthew 5:7).

Are you such a person? Are you merciful?

Discussion Questions

1. Saul tried to kill David on several occasions. Did he ever show remorse or ask David to show him mercy?

2. Recall an example of Jesus showing mercy to His enemies, even though they didn't ask for it.

3. Did you ever ask a close friend or family member for forgiveness? If you can, share that experience without breaking a confidence. Tell your group what happened and how you felt.

4. Have you ever shown mercy to someone who has died—a person who could no longer ask your forgiveness or hear you express it? Why be merciful in such a situation?

5. You may be reluctant to show mercy to someone for reasons such as these:

   - The person who offended you is still offending you.
   - The person who offended you is too proud to admit being wrong.
   - The person who offended you ought to be punished.
   - If you appear weak, your friends may desert you.
   - If you appear anxious to avoid conflict, others may take advantage of you.

6. Did David have any of these reasons to withhold mercy from Saul? If you are unwilling to forgive someone, what can you learn from David?

7. Saul's son Jonathan is not mentioned here, but how do you think he would have felt about his friend if he heard him forgive his father?

8. Think about your relationships with people you are likely to encounter this week. Do any of them need your mercy? How might you demonstrate mercy to them?

9. Do you believe you can forgive someone secretly without revealing your decision? Have you really forgiven someone if you're not willing to let that person know you have?

For Further Study

1. Jesus teaches us a great deal about forgiving our adversaries. Read the following passages and summarize Jesus' teachings in your own words.
   - Matthew 6:12–15
   - Matthew 18:21–35
   - Luke 6:37–38

2. The apostle Paul had an adversary in the church at Corinth who caused him a great deal of pain (2 Corinthians 2:5–11). What did he instruct the church to do about this person? Why?

GOD'S PROMISE FULFILLED
2 Samuel 5:1–13

What is a reasonable length of time to wait for a promise? If someone promises you a raise, or the use of a vacation home, or to marry you, when do you conclude that the promise is no good? If your best friend borrows a thousand dollars from you and promises to pay it back, how long is it before you think it's a broken promise? Five years? Ten? Twenty?

How long is one of God's promises good for? David was a young teenager when God promised him the throne of Israel, but decades have passed and David seems even less likely to become king than when he was a shepherd boy. He must be thinking, *Just what sort of promise is this?*

That's where we pick up the story. Word comes to David that Saul and Jonathan are dead, killed in battle. David grieves deeply and composes a song of sorrow. The chorus is a familiar phrase: *"How the mighty have fallen"* (2 Samuel 1:19, 25, 27). Have you ever used that phrase? Did you know its origin is an Old Testament song of grief?

As the grief wears off, it would only be natural for David to think, *Okay, now is the time for God to make good on His word.* So David asks God what he should do. *David said, "To which [city] shall I go up?" God said, "To Hebron"* (2 Samuel 2:1). Hebron is the capital of the southern kingdom known as Judah. It is just one state of the twelve tribes of Israel. It would be like God promising to make a man president of the United States, then saying, "Don't go to Washington, D.C. I want you to go to Montgomery, Alabama, and take charge of the Confederacy during the Civil War." That fulfills only half of what He promised. It would be like your cash-strapped friend saying, "I promised to repay you a thousand dollars but I only have five hundred, so take this." How would you feel about that?

And what kind of promise is one that creates nothing but trouble for you? David was promised the kingship and got a bloody civil war that lasted seven and a half years. What kind of promise is one that you have to fight for? Is that really a divine promise or something you have earned?

I don't know about you, but if I were in David's shoes I would start to think God had reneged on His word. I would feel like shouting, "This just isn't fair!" Yet we have no record of David reacting like that. He did as God instructed him, assumed the command of Hebron, and accepted the outcome without protest. Obviously, this fellow is maturing, both spiritually and emotionally.

THE WAR IS OVER—AND THE SOUTH HAS WON!

But wait a minute: The story's not over. We compared David's experience to the American Civil War, but his war has the opposite result. David's civil war comes to an end when elders of the tribes of Israel (the North) go to Hebron (the South) and say to him,

> *Look, we are your bone and flesh. For some time, while Saul was king over us, it was you who led out Israel and brought it in. The L*ORD *said to you: It is you who shall be shepherd of my people Israel, you who shall be ruler over Israel.* (2 Samuel 5:1–2)

They wanted David to be their king, too, so they asked permission to anoint him king over Israel. Now God's promise was made complete. *David was thirty years old when he began to reign, and he reigned forty years* (2 Samuel 5:4). He had to wait a long time for God's promise to be fulfilled, but so it was.

How long should you wait? It might depend on the circumstances. Perhaps you need a certain amount of maturing before you are ready to receive what God has for you. David did. Although life can be frustrating in the meantime, you will be better able to handle the promise when it finally arrives on your doorstep.

This was true of David. The first thing he does as king is brilliant. Instead of moving from Hebron, the capital of Judah, to Gibeah, the capital of Israel, David marches to a place smack-dab in the middle of the two, a city that was occupied by the Jebusites. This fortress city was so strong that the Jebusites laughed at David, saying, *"You will not come in here, even the blind and the lame will turn you back"* (2 Samuel 5:6). But David realized there was a weakness in defense of the city, an unguarded water shaft. To the surprise of the Jebusites, he conquers the city through its public water system. *David occupied the stronghold, and named it the city of David* (2 Samuel 5:9).

THE CITY OF DAVID

We know that expression, "the city of David." We hear it every year at Christmas. It's not Bethlehem, even though Luke uses that expression twice when telling us of Jesus' birth. Instead, the Old Testament refers to Jerusalem 46 different times as "the city of David." Jerusalem, a city created because of a promise, became the city of promise.

Jerusalem remains a place of incredible power and promise for the Jewish people—political, spiritual, and emotional promise. Every year, as Jewish people around the world end the Passover meal, their Seder benediction is, "Next year in Jerusalem." It is a place of promise created by God's promise to David, and it is the core of what being Jewish is about.

Jerusalem is also at the heart of the conflict in the Middle East. This became starkly apparent in the statements by Prime Minister Benjamin Netanyahu about the Iranian nuclear accord. "Extremists cannot be allowed to achieve their aims, not in Iran, not in Yemen and not in Jerusalem," he said, vowing that the city "will never be divided again."[5] Because Jerusalem was created by God's promise, Jews believe that any effort to deny Jerusalem's identity as the capital of Israel is to deny God's Word.

But for Christians, the promise of Jerusalem is even greater. After its destruction by the Romans in 70 AD, Jerusalem became not a temporal destination but an eternal one, not an earthly city but a heavenly city. So the last chapter of the Bible begins this way:

> *Then I saw a new heaven and a new earth; for the first heaven and the first earth had passed away, and the sea was no more. And I saw the holy city, the new Jerusalem, coming down out of heaven from God, prepared as a bride adorned for her husband. And I heard a loud voice from the throne saying,*
>
> *"See, the home of God is among mortals. He will dwell with them; they will be his peoples, and God himself will be with them; he will wipe every tear from their eyes. Death will be no more; mourning and crying and pain will be no more,*
> *for the first things have passed away." (Revelation 21: 1–4)*

Talk about a promise! How long do you wait for that promise? A lifetime. How long is the promise good for? Eternity.

GOD'S PROMISES TO YOU

The story of God's promise to David is filled with important spiritual truth for all of us because we are the people of His promises. God promises us an abundant and blessed life when we are in relationship with Him. God promises to sustain us no matter what life brings. God promises grace and love through Jesus Christ, no matter what we do, how we act, or who we are.

That all sounds well and good, but depending on the circumstance of your life, you might find yourself wondering if God is good for it. You may be saying, "If I'm promised an abundant and blessed life, then where is it? If God is going to sustain and strengthen me during every circumstance, then why is life so tough and difficult at times? What's going on?"

Life would be easier if the time between God's promise and its fulfillment was always short, but David would tell us that simply isn't the way God works. We have to wait. Waiting is hard, particularly when the circumstances of waiting are difficult and uncertain. But David would also say we can't wait passively. We have to be faithful to God while we are waiting. We must have a heart for God and the courage to face our giants. We must offer love to our brothers and sisters, mercy and grace to those who wrong us. Even though doubt may raise its head (and we know it will), we need to remember that God is for us. David did all of these things for half of a lifetime, actively waiting for God's promise to be fulfilled. In the end, *David then perceived that the L*ORD *had established him king over Israel, and that he had exalted his kingdom for the sake of his people Israel* (2 Samuel 5:12).

In the end, David learned that God's promise was true. And in the end, that's what we must believe. Our faith is in God. God knows how to accomplish what He promises us. God will deliver what He has promised in the fullness of time—not just in our lifetime, but in the next time. Though the promise of eternal life and the assurance of hope in the New Jerusalem are great and precious, we can trust God to make them complete.

Discussion Questions

1. How did God communicate His promise to the boy David that he would become king of Israel? Had God sent anyone else to affirm that promise since then?

2. A long-standing legal maxim says, "Justice delayed is justice denied." Recall times when God's people felt they had suffered under injustice for too long. Did they say this disproved God's promises, or did they reaffirm those promises when they prayed for help?

3. When you find yourself waiting for God to fulfill a promise in your life, what do you think about? What do you do?

4. Describe a promise that God has fulfilled in your life. How long did you have to wait for it?

5. What is another promise that God has not yet fulfilled in your life?

6. How might you verify that a delayed promise is truly from God, and that you understand it correctly?

For Further Study

1. Compare how God called David (1 Samuel 16:1–13), Samuel (1 Samuel 3:1–18), and Isaiah (Isaiah 6:1–6). God revealed His promise to these men in three different ways. Which would have been most convincing to you? Has God ever revealed a promise to you in one of those ways?

2. Review God's promises to David's ancestors Abraham (Genesis 22:15–18) and Isaac (Genesis 26:2–5). In light of the eventual division and defeat of their nation, do you think God failed to keep His promises to them? Do you think God decided not to keep those promises because the Jews turned away from Him?

3. Reflect on God's promises concerning your loved ones who have died (1 Thessalonians 4:13–14; 5:10; 9—10; Revelation 14:12–13). Which of these promises encourage you most?

PASSIONS, GOOD AND BAD
2 Samuel 6

I must warn you: Some things about this chapter will be troubling. We will encounter morally unclear motives, questionable decisions, disregard for human life, and violence. Why? Because David's story is drawn from real life. That's what makes it so instructive for each of us. Let's recap what we have learned so far:

David was just a young shepherd in the hills of Judah when he was anointed by Samuel to become the next king of Israel. But God wasn't in any hurry to fulfill the promise. David finally became king at age thirty—of Judah—only one of the twelve tribes of Israel. A bloody civil war broke out between Judah and Israel. After seven and a half years, the war ended and David finally became the king over the entire nation. In his first act as king, he marches on Mount Zion, a Jebusite stronghold strategically located between Israel and Judah. He captures the stronghold and declares it his capital, which gives it the reputation of being the City of David. It is now commonly known as Jerusalem.

From that point, a subtle but substantial shift takes place in the life of David. He's no longer the shepherd boy who would be king or the marauding chieftain, fighting for his little state. He trades in his military clothes for regal dress and begins acting like the kings of other nations. For example, he greets ambassadors from other countries. "Hiram, king of Tyre sent messengers to David, along with cedar trees, and carpenters, and masons who built David a house" (2 Samuel 5:11). All of this feels really good to David. He looks around and says, "Look how God has exalted me."

DAVID'S PASSION FOR WOMEN

How does Lord Acton's expression go? "Power tends to corrupt and absolute power corrupts absolutely."6 Suddenly, we see David acting like a tenth-century king with a strong army and an opulent palace. The only thing missing is a harem, *so after he came from Hebron, David took more concubines and wives; and more sons and daughters were born to David* (2 Samuel 5:13). Now the questionable moral decisions begin, or perhaps it would be fairer to say they increase. To see this, we need to go back and pick up another thread of David's story.

Scripture says that David's first wife was Michal, the daughter of King Saul. Michal loved David and wanted to marry him, but Saul would allow it only if David brought him the foreskins of 100 Philistines. This was really a scheme to get David killed in battle. But David didn't bring back just 100 trophies; he brought back 200 and the marriage was on (1 Samuel 18:25–27).

David's problems with King Saul became a problem with the marriage. When David ran for his life, he left Michal behind and took two other women to be his wives. King Saul then gave Michal to another man (1 Samuel 25). Once David become king of Judah, he loved Michal enough to demand her return, which separated her from her new husband (2 Samuel 3:12–15). But David didn't love her enough to make her his only wife. In Hebron, David added six wives who gave him six sons.

Does it bother you that David had so many wives? Well, once he gets into his fancy palace David decides he needs more, even though this is clearly going against the law found in Deuteronomy. It said that the king *must not acquire many wives for himself, or else his heart will turn away; also silver and gold he must not acquire in great quantity for himself* (Deuteronomy 17:17). David's passion for women was wrong, but he indulged it anyway. All told, David now had eight wives and twenty children (nineteen sons and one daughter), not counting children sired with his concubines. Would you be surprised if I told you that big family problems are ahead? The sexual politics and sin of David's passions will come back to haunt him.

DAVID'S PASSION FOR POWER

I think you've got the picture: a palace, a harem, a citadel city with a large army, and ambassadors from nations showing up and paying homage. But David looks around and thinks something else is missing. What is it? And then it comes to him—the Ark of the Covenant.

Most of what today's readers know about the Ark of the Covenant comes from the esteemed Dr. Henry Jones, the daring archeologist known to moviegoers as "Indiana Jones." While much of what he and friend Steven Spielberg said about the Ark was true, Indiana Jones didn't have it completely right.

God gave Moses instructions to build the Ark of the Covenant complete with measurements, directions to decorate it, and very clear instructions on how to transport it. Moses placed the stone tablets of the Ten Commandments in it and believed that the Ark was the locus of God's presence (Exodus 25:10–16). The Ark became the place of God's self-revelation, so that Moses would hear the voice of

God coming from between the two golden cherubim sitting on the top of the Ark (Exodus 25:17–22). The Ark helped lead the Israelites from Sinai to the Promised Land and parted the Jordan River as they crossed (Joshua 3). Then the Ark functioned as a powerful weapon in the siege of Jericho. The priests carried it around Jericho seven days in a row, trumpets blasting, scaring the residents to death. On the seventh day, the Ark made seven circuits of the city; then the Israelites shouted and the walls of Jericho came tumbling down (Joshua 6).

The Ark was perceived as being so powerful the Philistines actually captured it and tried to use it for their own purposes. But instead of harnessing its power, they found it kept toppling the icon of their god, Dagon. They finally gave it back (1 Samuel 5).

So where was the Ark of the Covenant now? Unlike in *Indiana Jones*, the Israelites had not stored it away in some warehouse. It was actually at the house of a Levite priest named Abinadab and his two priestly sons, Uzzah and Ahio. For twenty years, it had been collecting dust because King Saul really didn't have any use for it or God.

The way David goes about retrieving the Ark reveals his motive. *David again gathered all the chosen men of Israel, thirty thousand. David and all the people with him set out and went from Baale-judah, to bring up from there the Ark of God* (2 Samuel 6:1–2a). Why go get the Ark with thirty thousand men? That was an army. Was David afraid the Ark might be captured en route? Hardly. David had just defeated the Philistines and they didn't want the Ark anyway. They'd given it back years ago. No, this isn't about protection; it's about politics. Bringing the Ark from a place of storage to his new capital was a powerful propaganda effort to assert that David's new regime was blessed by God.[7] In effect, David's great procession was his way of saying, "God's on my side, at my capital, and if you want to see

God, you've got to come to my place in Jerusalem." This is not about a passion for God; it's an attempt to legitimize his power as king. And the attempt backfires on him.

WHAT'S WRONG WITH THIS PICTURE?

Remember, God had given very clear instructions about the Ark, including how it was to be transported. David ignored those instructions. Instead of having the priests slide poles through the rings on the side of the Ark and carrying it reverently, they just threw it onto an ox cart. There was nothing reverent about it. Theirs was a noisy military parade complete with a band banging tambourines, drums, and cymbals. Half way to Jerusalem, at the threshing floor of Nacon, Uzzah reached out and took hold of the Ark of God because the oxen stumbled.

> *The LORD's anger burned against Uzzah because of his irreverent act; therefore God struck him down and he died there beside the ark of God.* (2 Samuel 6:6–7)

It's not unusual for a narrator to kill off a minor character, but really! Why would God strike down a member of the honor guard who's just trying to avoid a mishap? Really, God? Really?

There are some mean streets in the Bible—ones we don't want to go down—and unfortunately, we just found one. What do we do with this? It's the kind of Bible passage that caused Mark Twain to say of God, "If he had had a motto, it would have read, 'Let no innocent person escape.'"[8] That seems true of poor Uzzah. What did he do to deserve this?

Even though we might not like the answer, the answer is important. Remember Uzzah was a priest and he should have known better than to throw the Ark of the Covenant on an ox cart. But his spontaneous gesture revealed much more—Uzzah was no longer awed by the Ark or the least bit fearful of God's power. He assumed God was so impotent that if the box fell, God fell. He thought God was so weak that God needed his help to make it down the street. He may even have found humor in the idea that God was trapped inside a fragile religious symbol that they had just dusted off to use in this parade.[9] Uzzah didn't respect the power of God and paid the ultimate price.

As Bible scholar Walter Brueggemann aptly notes, "When people are no longer awed, respectful, or fearful of God's holiness, the community is put at risk."[10] David is using the Ark for his own purposes, seeing it as religious equipment to further his political agenda. David doesn't respect God's power, and that is deadly. His lack of respect is revealed by his reaction: He becomes angry and curses God. It is a wonder that God doesn't strike him too. David suddenly realizes this and becomes afraid. He leaves the Ark right there and high-tails it back to Jerusalem, putting himself into a spiritual time-out.

A PASSION FOR WORSHIP

Three months later, David is ready to try it again, but everything is different. There is no mention of an army of thirty thousand men, no percussive military parade, and no ox cart. They reverently carry the Ark as prescribed by God. When they have taken six steps, David stops and sacrifices a bull and a fattened calf. This time it's not passionate propaganda; it's passionate worship. David strips down, literally and figuratively, baring himself before God. Then,

David danced before the LORD with all his might; David was girded with a linen ephod. So David and all the house of Israel brought up the ark of the LORD with shouting, and with the sound of the trumpet. (2 Samuel 6:14–15)

In ninety days, David has gone from disdain for the power of God to passionate, awe-inspiring worship before God. He is lost in ecstatic praise of God, putting all of his energy and being into dancing before God. It is a liturgical dance, passionately expressing praise for God's power. But can you imagine jumping, leaping, and dancing in praise of God in nothing more than a linen loincloth, a whirling dervish honoring God? Would you be comfortable with that worship style? Doing it? Watching it? Be honest. Not everyone is, because:

As the ark of the LORD came into the city of David, Michal daughter of Saul looked out of the window, and saw King David leaping and dancing before the LORD; and she despised him in her heart. (2 Samuel 6:16)

There she is again, David's first wife, Michal. Why did she despise him for the way he was worshiping? Perhaps you have been uncomfortable with someone else's worship style. It happens often, then and now. But there is more here than meets the eye, more than opinions about worship style.

David returned to bless his household. But Michal daughter of Saul came out to meet David, and said, "How the king of Israel honored himself today, uncovering himself today before the eyes of his servants' maids, as any vulgar fellow might shamelessly uncover himself!" (2 Samuel 6:20)

She sees David's sexual passions out of control again. Can we blame her? When someone has betrayed you, it is hard to look beyond the betrayal. Sadly, with this interchange, the relationship between David and Michal is irrevocably broken. The chapter comes to a close with the suggestion that they never shared a bed again, for *Michal daughter of Saul had no children to the day of her death* (2 Samuel 6:23).

PASSIONS OF OUR OWN

Wow, what a read! You can see why I warned you. We are left with lots of questions about the life of David, but also about our own lives. Let me share a few of these questions for you to ponder in your own spiritual "time-out":

Do I ever take God's power for granted or treat God's holiness causally?

Do I always come before God with honor and respect?

Is my passion for power more important than my passion for God?

Do I judge and criticize others for the way they worship God?

The power of God is real and deserves our constant respect. Not respecting God's power can be spiritually deadly. As a result, the way we treat the things of God is critical to our spiritual walk.

David eventually got it right, worshiping God passionately with all his might. What he didn't get right were his carnal passions. They opened a rift in David's family that was about to crumble.

Discussion Questions

1. Make a list of David's most obvious character qualities before he became king and after he became king. What do you suppose accounts for the difference?

2. What evidence suggests that David still had the qualities that distinguished him as a boy and young man?

3. Imagine you are David's first wife, Michal, and you genuinely loved him before you were married. What events changed your view of him?

4. The title of this chapter ("Passions, Good and Bad") suggests that some passions contribute to the health of another individual, family, or community while other passions tend to weaken or destroy them. Arrange these human passions into two lists, according to those two different outcomes: beauty, community, envy, generosity, gluttony, greed, health, independence, jealousy, lust, peace-making, pride, solitude, spiritual growth.

Helathy Passions	Harmful Passions

5. What members of your group seem to be the most passionate? What are they passionate about?

6. Other group members may feel just as passionate about pursuing certain goals, although their fervor is not obvious. How might you encourage them to express their passions?

For Further Study

1. Find proof of this statement in David's life: "The passions we express shape our *reputation*; the passions we control shape our *character*."

2. Now find proof of that statement in your own life.

THE TRAP OF SELF-RIGHTEOUSNESS
2 Samuel 11:26—12:7, 13

What kind of books do you like to take on your summer vacation? "Beach read" preferences are varied. Some like getting lost in a fantasy while others enjoy a suspenseful thriller; some like historical fiction while others want the most popular beach read genre, romance.

There is nothing romantic about the next chapter of David's life, but it does have other ingredients that characterize most "beach reads": lust, sex, and murder. Indeed, this is one of the most infamous chapters of David's life. He had "a heart for God" but, like all of us, he was vulnerable to sin. As with everything else in his daring life, David sinned boldly and without hesitation.

We have seen that David finally became king of Israel at age forty. He established his capital at Jerusalem, built a palace for himself, and brought the Ark of the Covenant into the city. Tragically, he also collected multiple wives and concubines even though Deuteronomy 17:17 said the king should not do this. This revealed an addictive tendency in our hero's life, which would cause him to hit rock bottom ten years later.

GREATER THAN A TEMPLE

David proposed to do something that seemed quite noble and God-honoring, but indirectly it led to his moral failure: He proposed to build a temple for the Ark of the Covenant. God, however, said through the prophet Nathan, *"No. I have something greater in mind."* Nathan then foretold that David's family would reign forever, a kingdom without end (2 Samuel 7:8–16).

This promise of a dynasty for David's family came with an incredible statement of grace. Until this moment, the relationship between God and God's people was conditional for blessing and mercy. It depended upon Israel's obedience, the "if" of Exodus 19. God had said, *"Now therefore, if you obey my voice and keep my covenant, you shall be my treasured possession"* (Exodus 19:5). But with David, God shifts from the conditional "if" to a grace-filled "but":

> *But I will not take my steadfast love from him, as I took it from Saul, whom I put away from before you. Your house and your kingdom shall be made sure forever before me.* (2 Samuel 7:15–16)

This was a game-changing promise and David accepted it without hesitation. God promised to bless David forever despite his sin. Of course, the nation of Israel didn't last forever, even though it had an incredible run of nearly four hundred years. So what kind of a promise was this?

We asked that question a couple of chapters ago how long God's promises are good, and the answer is still the same. One thousand years after God makes this promise to David, it is affirmed by the angel named Gabriel. Do you remember what he said to Mary?

> *You will conceive in your womb and bear a son, and you will name him Jesus. He will be great, and will be called the Son of*

the Most High, and the Lord God will give to him the throne of his ancestor David. He will reign over the house of Jacob forever, and of his kingdom there will be no end. (Luke 1:31–33)

How long is God's promise good? Forever. For eternity. The enduring promise God makes to David gives birth to the hope for a Messiah and the unconditional love and grace we have in Jesus.

WHAT WAS DAVID THINKING?

It is hard to know if David perceived God's unconditional love and grace in the prophecy of 2 Samuel 7. It's really hard to know what he was thinking in the sordid events that follow, but scripture indicates that he was motivated by lust.

He saw from the roof a woman bathing; the woman was very beautiful. David sent someone to inquire about the woman. It was reported, "This is Bathsheba daughter of Eliam, the wife of Uriah the Hittite." (2 Samuel 11:2–3)

Even though David was told this woman was married to one of his soldiers, he dispatched his servants to get her.

What was he thinking? He wasn't. Lust is notorious for obliterating common sense in the most sensible people. Studies suggest that the brain in this phase is much like a brain on drugs. MRI scans illustrate that the same area lights up when an addict gets a fix of cocaine as when experiencing the intense lust of physical attraction.[11] Lust can be an addiction, and it clearly was for David.

Notice how this goes down: *So David sent messengers to get her, and she came to him, and he lay with her.... Then she returned to her house* (2 Samuel 11:4). I told you this is no romance. There are no flowers, no wining and dining, no dancing in the moonlight, not even an exchange of names. He sent; he took; he lay. There is no hint of caring or affection for this woman, only lust. The author of this "beach read" isn't getting paid by the words either. The next verse says, *The woman conceived; and she sent and told David, "I am pregnant"* (v 5). The impersonal isn't even dignified at this point in the story with a name; she simply says, "I am pregnant."

A common plot turn at this point in a blockbuster novel is the cover-up, and the cover-up is always worse than the crime. We may not call this story "Bathsheba-gate," but David concocted a cover-up worse than the one that drove President Nixon from office.

Without hesitation, David sent word to his general, Joab, on the front line to have the soldier Uriah sent to him. So Uriah came. It must have felt odd for a foot soldier to give the king a military briefing. ("How's General Joab? How is the army? How goes the war?"). Then David, probably wrapping his arm around Uriah or giving him a wink, said, *"Go down to your house, and wash your feet"* (2 Samuel 11:8). Now that may seem like an odd expression to you; but between two ancient soldiers, this locker room talk was well understood. It meant, "Go sleep with your wife; enjoy the pleasure of her company." So David told Uriah to "wash his feet" before he went back to the front line. It's a bold yet simple cover-up strategy.

"Beach read" cover-ups seldom work the way they are designed, and this is no exception. Even though David encouraged Uriah to go down to his house, Uriah didn't go. He slept outside the palace with David's servants that night.

David's intelligence network reported this, so David brought Uriah back in. Why didn't he go and "wash his feet" with his wife? A sex addict like David couldn't imagine a soldier not "washing his feet," particularly with a woman like Uriah's wife. But for Uriah, this was unthinkable. He said:

> "The ark and Israel and Judah remain in booths; and my lord Joab and the servants of my lord are camping in the open field; shall I then go to my house, to eat and to drink, and to lie with my wife? As you live, and as your soul lives, I will not do such a thing." (2 Samuel 11:11)

Without hesitation, David came up with a second plan. He invited Uriah to spend one more night at Jerusalem and proceeded to get Uriah drunk, thinking the alcohol would put Uriah in the mood for love. It didn't work.

IF ALL ELSE FAILS, MURDER

It is frightening to see how quickly David came up with a third strategy to keep his house of cards from falling. He wrote a letter to Joab, ordering him to put Uriah at the front of the line where the fighting was fiercest and then withdraw. Brazenly, he gave the letter to Uriah himself to carry back to the general, and Joab executed the order. *Some of the servants of David among the people fell. Uriah the Hittite was killed as well* (2 Samuel 11:17).

Joab felt guilty, not only for the death of Uriah but for others in the army. He worried about repercussions for himself. So when Joab sent a messenger back to the king, he said in essence, "Tell him about the battle. Tell how bad I feel about the casualties. But don't tell him Uriah is dead until the very end."

David could care less about the battle. He wanted to hear only one thing. Finally, he did: "Uriah the Hittite is dead." David's response was nothing short of appalling.

> *David said to the messenger, "Thus you shall say to Joab, 'Do not let this matter trouble you, for the sword devours now one and now another'.... And encourage him."* (2 Samuel 11:25, 26)

David set himself up as a moral authority, comforting Joab for his participation in the cover-up. "War is war," he says with a shrug. "These things happen. There is bound to be some collateral damage. Don't let it get you down, Joab." David rationalized murder, not just of Uriah but also of other loyal soldiers, to sustain his cover-up. He told his general that such things were necessary for the good of the nation.[12]

The ugly chapter ends this way: *When the mourning was over, David sent and brought her to his house, and she became his wife, and bore him a son* (2 Samuel 11:27). Note there is still no name for this woman. She is still a nameless "she," just something to take.

David's acts are willful, committed without hesitation. He didn't stumble into sin. He was a decisive leader and a decisive, premeditated sinner. Now David has truly hit rock-bottom. It started with lust, became adultery, and then turned into murder, not just of one but of many.

For eight or nine months, David thinks he has gotten away with murder. His house of cards is still standing. *But the thing that David had done displeased the LORD* (v 27). Sin always displeases God and there are always consequences to sin, whether great or small.

CAUGHT IN A STORY

Enter Nathan again. Nathan was the prophet who had spoken on God's behalf when God promised to bless David with a dynasty, a kingdom that would last forever. To say that David and Nathan had a close relationship is an understatement. He had the king's ear because he spoke God's truth to David. David had to listen.

"David," Nathan says. "I have a story to tell you." He told of a rich man who had everything, including many flocks of sheep and herds of goats. Nearby there was a poor man who only had one little female lamb, which he loved like a daughter. It would eat with him, drink with him, and rest on his chest like a baby. One day, the rich man needed dinner for a visitor. But instead of taking a lamb from his own huge flock, he took the poor man's lamb, and prepared that for the guest who had come to him.

> *Then David's anger was greatly kindled against the man. He said to Nathan, "As the LORD lives, the man who has done this deserves to die; he shall restore the lamb fourfold, because he did this thing, and because he had no pity." Nathan said to David, "You are the man!"* (2 Samuel 12:5–7)

David's response is nothing short of remarkable. Without hesitation David says, *I have sinned against the Lord.* A lesser man, certainly the type of fictional characters we encounter in most "beach reads," would simply have killed the prophet. Instead, David confesses. He knows he is guilty. He has sinned against God. So Nathan said to David:

> *Now the Lord has put away your sin; you shall not die. Nevertheless, because by this deed you have utterly scorned the LORD, the child that is born to you shall die.* (2 Samuel 12:14)

God forgave David but didn't excuse him from the consequences of his behavior. There are always consequences. In this case, there would be short-term consequences (the child illicitly conceived will die) and long-term consequences (David's sin of lust will spread like a cancer in his family for generations). What a tragedy! When God blessed David more than anybody, the king seemed to think he lived above the law. Not so. God would not excuse David's sinful behavior.

SEEING OURSELVES IN DAVID'S STORY

There are a lot of different ways we can read this terrible, sad chapter in the life of David. We can get so caught up in the theology and history and moral inconsistencies that we totally miss what this story is all about. We can so identify with one character and the terrible injustices he or she suffers that we can only feel pity for that person. Or we may just wish this story wasn't in the Bible, because it makes us so uncomfortable to see the way David acts—and, for that matter, the way God acts.

For all of these reasons, we may miss the point: This story is a mirror image of ourselves. It reminds us that we can easily see the sins of others while self-righteously ignoring our own. We can justify and rationalize our behavior so that something that is grossly sinful seems acceptable and right. You've done that. I've done that. Whether we want to accept it or not, David's story shows us ourselves.

Because this story is a mirror image of our own behavior, we need to respond as David did. Without hesitation, we need to confess: *I have sinned against the LORD* (2 Samuel 12:13). If we confess our sins, God will forgive us. That is the amazing grace God offers to you, to me, and to David.[13]

The story ends in an amazing way. The child dies. There is terrible grief. *Then David consoled his wife Bathsheba [note she now has a name], and went to her, and lay with her; and she bore a son, and he named him Solomon. The LORD loved him* (2 Samuel 12:24).

Solomon's birth is a stunner worthy of any great "beach read." David and Bathsheba's relationship started in sin. Their marriage should never have happened because David killed her husband. Nevertheless, God brought life into death, offered grace after judgment, and sustained the promise made to David and to us.

So David's story is both a warning and blessing to us. It calls us to be alert to our self-rationalizing sin. It warns us that there will be consequences to our sinful actions. And it reminds us of the amazing, life-giving grace offered by God when we confess our sin. Powerful truths from a powerful "read"!

Discussion Questions

1. Why do you suppose stories containing violence, sexual promiscuity, and deceit are included in the Bible?

2. Does David's blatant sin make it easier for you to see yourself in his story, or more difficult? Why?

3. Do you see evidence that David consulted with Nathan or any of his close advisers before he decided what to do about Bathsheba and Uriah? What can we learn from this?

4. We hear from Bathsheba only once in this story, when she tells David she is pregnant. Express how she might have felt about David (a) when he summoned her to have sex with him, (b) when he arranged her husband's death, and (c) when he married her to conceal their illicit sex. What might have happened to Bathsheba if she resisted David at any of these points?

5. Do you believe a religious person is more likely to sin without realizing it? Why or why not?

6. Nathan's confrontation of David is a good example of "speaking truth to power."[14] What other examples do you see in the Bible? In recent history?

7. What are some effective ways to "speak truth to power" when the person in power was chosen by God?

For Further Study

1. Compare God's promise to David (2 Samuel 7:16) with His promise to Mary (Luke 1:33–35). How has Jesus fulfilled these promises?

2. In what sense are these promises yet to be fulfilled? (Revelation 22:1–5).

LIKE FATHER, LIKE SON—BUT WORSE!
2 Samuel 13:1–2, 6–8, 11–16, 28; 14:28–33

    Have you ever watched what you thought was a reasonable, normal family suddenly fall apart? Maybe they were your neighbors down the street. For all intents and purposes, they looked like the average Joe and Jane Doe, a nice family with two kids and a puppy dog. With your interactions in the front yard and at holiday neighborhood gatherings, they appeared to be a happy, upstanding, well-adjusted family. But late one night, flashing lights of squad cars appear in front of their house. To the surprise of everyone on the block, one of Joe and Jane's kids is in trouble with the law. Or an argument has led to a rather loud and disquieting event of domestic violence. From the outside, this family looked so right. But in reality, they were dysfunctional.

    To many, King David's family appeared fine, but the reality was different. Over the years, seeds of conflict, abuse, and lawlessness were sown, and the consequences were felt by Israel for generations. We seldom see the beginning of the brokenness that creates a dysfunctional family system. But with David's family, we see signs of it well before the royal dysfunction moves into the public's eye.

EARLY SIGNS OF DYSFUNCTION

The first seed likely came in David's first marriage to Michal. David won her hand by presenting King Saul trophies of 200 emasculated Philistine soldiers. When Saul became jealous of David's military victories, he threatened murder. David ran for his life and King Saul gave Michal to another man.

Michal and David were reunited at age thirty when David became the King of Judah. Perhaps their relationship had been damaged by their separation, or maybe David thought it was a kingly thing to do at the time, or most likely because David was sexually addicted—whatever the reason, David started adding other wives. Michal may have moved back home but she did not receive his undivided attention. I think most of us would expect polygamy to be a recipe for dysfunction. David's six wives give birth to six sons in seven-and-one-half years. Two of the first three sons are principal characters in the drama that will unfold in this chapter, revealing the depth of David's royal dysfunction:

> *These are the sons of David who were born to him in Hebron: the firstborn was Amnon, by Ahinoam the Jezreelite; the second Daniel, by Abigail the Carmelite; the third Absalom, son of Maacah, daughter of King Talmai of Geshur.* (1 Chronicles 3:1–2a)

For this episode, Amnon and Absalom are the two to remember. We don't know what happened to Daniel. Perhaps he died or did something disgraceful that got him written out of the story. (Families are that way. You may have a relative or two who just disappear from your genealogy). At any rate, Amnon was the firstborn and first in line for the throne, while somehow Absalom became second in line. We also know that Absalom had a sister named Tamar who was incredibly beautiful. She is David's only daughter named in scripture.

By the time David became king of Jerusalem, Michal despised David with all her heart. When a marriage is broken, children suffer. Michal and David's relationship was so fractured that they had no children, but the children of his other wives observed their spitefulness and contentiousness.

An unresolved, unnamed conflict is like a cancer growing in any family. This cancer's growth was accelerated by the behavior of David at age fifty, which we saw unfold in the previous chapter. David's boys Ammon and Absalom, each nearly twenty years old, watched it too: David saw an incredibly beautiful woman bathing and was filled with lust. As we noted before, lust obliterates common sense in the most sensible people. Even though the woman was married to one of his soldiers, David took her into his bed; then summarily sent her away. To his shock and dismay, she became pregnant.

He unsuccessfully tried to cover it up, finally resorting to murder by sending the woman's husband back to the front line of battle carrying his own death sentence in a handwritten message to general Joab. David thought he'd gotten away with it, but one never gets away with such things. There are always consequences. In this chapter, David must come to grips with the fact that *you reap whatever you sow* (Galatians 6:7).

HIS FATHER'S SON

Have you ever noticed that children seldom do what you tell them to do? Instead they do what they see you doing; they imitate the behavior you have modeled for them. A few years after David modeled lust, infidelity, and murder, his firstborn son does the same. It starts this way. *David's son Absalom had a beautiful sister whose name was Tamar; and David's son Amnon fell in love with her* (2 Samuel 13:1). Remember, Amnon is the number-one prince. He thinks he is in love with his half-sister, Tamar, but it is not really love; it's lust. We see this in the very next verse:

> *Amnon was so tormented that he made himself ill because of his sister Tamar, for she was a virgin and it seemed impossible to Amnon to do anything to her.* (2 Samuel 13:2)

Wanting "to do anything to her" is physical; it is lust. If the family had been healthy and Amnon hadn't seen his father's lecherous behavior, it might have ended there; however, a cunning, inventive cousin by the name of Jonadab comes up with a plan for Amnon's desire to be fulfilled. "Act like you're sick," he says, "then ask your dad to let Tamar be your nurse" (v 5). So Ammon goes to bed and pretends to be ill. He then asks his father David to send Tamar to his bedside to feed and nurse him back to health. David agrees. Ironically, like Uriah, David himself carries the message to her and unwittingly aids in what unfolds[15] (v 7).

Tamar goes to Amnon's home, where she prepares cakes and takes them to him to eat. He grabs her and says, *"Come, lie with me, my sister."* She answers, *"No, my brother, do not force me...do not do anything so vile!"* (2 Samuel 13:11–12). She tries and tries to reason with him to defuse the situation. She clearly says no!

> *But he would not listen to her; and being stronger than she, he forced her and lay with her. Then Amnon was seized with a very great loathing for her; indeed, his loathing was even greater than the lust he had felt for her. Amnon said to her, "Get out!"* (2 Samuel 13:14–15)

Where did he learn to act like this? From his father. Amnon is so filled with lust he can't control himself. He rapes Tamar and then sends her away in disgrace. Unlike Bathsheba, Tamar will not cover up what happens. As she leaves Amnon's home, she makes a public gesture of humiliation by ripping her clothes to show she is no longer a virgin and putting ashes on her head in mourning. The entire neighborhood now knows of the royal dysfunction. They witness more of the same because, *When King David heard of all these things, he became very angry, but he would not punish his son Amnon, because he loved him, for he was his firstborn* (2 Samuel 13:21). It's unbelievable. David did nothing about his son's heinous behavior. It's the kind of thing that sickens me about a novel. When characters are so reprehensible that they appear unredeemable, I will put the book down. But this isn't a novel; it's the Bible, so we press on.

A BROTHER'S REVENGE

David did nothing, but not Absalom. *Absalom hated Amnon, because he had raped his sister Tamar* (2 Samuel 13:22), and he began to plot revenge against his brother. Two years later, Absalom sees his chance. He decides to act at an annual festival to celebrate sheep shearing. Absalom tries to get David to attend the festival's banquet as the honored guest. When it is clear that David will not come, Absalom asks that Amnon be sent instead. David is suspicious, but finally sends Amnon in his place. Since it will be a big party, all the other sons of David go, too. Absalom puts together a feast fit for a king and everyone is really enjoying himself. *Then Absalom commanded his servants, "Watch when Amnon's heart is merry with wine, and when I say to you, 'Strike Amnon,' then kill him. Do not be afraid; have I not myself commanded you? Be courageous and valiant"* (2 Samuel 13:28). That is exactly what they do.

Once Amnon is drunk, servants kill the heir to the throne while sitting at the banquet table. Can you imagine the panic, the chaos? Then you won't be surprised to learn that all of the other princes fear wholesale slaughter, so they run for their lives.

Word of the royal dysfunction travels fast, but it somehow gets exaggerated and the messenger tells David that Absalom has indeed killed every one of the king's sons. The weight of this news is unbearable. David tears his clothes, falls on the ground, and grieves. Into this tragic scene, back comes cousin Jonadab, who devised the scheme that Amnon used to rape Tamar. He says to David, *"Amnon alone is dead. This has been determined by Absalom from the day Amnon raped his sister Tamar"* (2 Samuel 13:32). Sure enough, coming down the road, riding their mules, are all the sons of David—except Absalom. Absalom flees to the hill country of Geshur, his grandfather's home, where he stays for three years.

This awful chapter ends with these words: *David mourned for his son day after day* (2 Samuel 13:37). Which son is he weeping for, the dead Amnon or the banished Absalom? We aren't told. Maybe David doesn't know.

WE REAP WHAT WE SOW

At this point, I wonder whether David connects the facts and realizes that he'd created the monstrous behavior by his two sons. Do you think he said, "Amnon just did what I did, and so did Absalom. I did all of this, modeled this royal dysfunction. Because of my own behavior I have lost a son to murder, a daughter to rape, and another son to fratricide. I sowed these seeds." Do you suppose he grasped this? Whether he realized it or not, David had set the pattern for his family and it wasn't going to get any easier for him.

Some parts of David's story are just wonderful, and we love for our children to hear them—like the episode of a little shepherd boy bringing down a big, bad giant with nothing but a sling shot. Then we come to awful events like this. We want to put our hands over our children's ears, even our own ears. Why do we have all this dysfunctional stuff in the Bible?

I'll tell you why: The Bible is about real lives and real people like you and me. It is fair to say that we all have some secrets behind the doors of our homes, some heart-wrenching challenges, even some damaging, sinful things. We need to learn from David to deal with these things sooner, not later. We can't just let dysfunctional behavior go. If we do, it will become a cancer that grows and grows until it destroys our lives.

That sounds rather fatalistic, but it doesn't have to be, because a second truth is this: Personal behavior can impact future generations for good as well as bad. If we do good, we can reap a wonderful harvest.

> *Do not be deceived; God is not mocked, for you reap whatever you sow.... So let us not grow weary in doing what is right, for we will reap at harvest time, if we do not give up. So then, whenever we have an opportunity, let us work for the good of all, and especially for those of the family of faith.* (Galatians 6:7, 9–10)

Take this lesson out of David's terrible story: The seeds you sow are important—they last for generations—so plant carefully and don't let any bad seeds take root. Address brokenness and sin immediately. I'm sure that, in hindsight, David wished he had embraced this truth.

If only I could tell you things will all be better in the next chapter! But I can't. Royal dysfunction will turn into royal treason. There will be brokenness, death, and loss. David's story is a tragic Bible "beach read," but it also is God's story. While it is difficult to see in this chapter, God's plan is surely unfolding and will become clearer before David's story ends.

Discussion Questions

1. In what we've read so far, what events suggest that David was sexually addicted?

2. How do a man's descendants usually become aware of his sexual sins?

3. Do you think people are more likely to repeat the sexual sins of their parents without realizing it is sin? Why or why not?

4. How might David have stopped the dysfunctions of promiscuity and revenge in his family?

5. What influences in today's culture make sexual sin seem to be acceptable?

6. What can you do to counteract these influences in your children's lives?

7. What ministries of your congregation could combat these influences?

For Further Study

1. Solomon was born to David and Bathsheba after their illegitimate son died (2 Samuel 12:24), yet he said that his father walked before God "in faithfulness, in righteousness, and in uprightness of heart" (1 Kings 3:6). Do you think he was just boasting? Why or why not?

2. The Old Testament gives us plenty of evidence that "you reap whatever you sow" (Galatians 6:7). Look up the following two examples. In each case, note the *seed* (the sin of the ancestor) and the *fruit* (the sin of the descendant). Cain and Lamech (Genesis 4:1–10, 17–24); Abram and Jacob (Genesis 12:10–20; 27:1–17).

Seed	Fruit

PARALYZED BY GRIEF

2 Samuel 18:9–15, 24, 31–33

The two previous chapters have given us a great deal of sex and murder. This chapter of David's life is a political drama, yet no less tragic than what has preceded this. We saw in the previous chapter that King David's third son Absalom killed the crown prince Amnon, apparently to avenge the rape of his sister Tamar. But human motives are often mixed, and Absalom might have had something else in mind when he murdered his brother.

Absalom spends three years in exile. Then, General Joab secures permission from King David to bring his son home because *the king's heart longed for Absalom* (2 Samuel 14:1 NIV). But when Absalom returns, David refuses to see him. Reconciliation can be slow and painful, especially when families have tragic losses to overcome. When one family member does harm to another, forgiveness can seem impossible to give.

At end of two years of living in Jerusalem, Absalom has had enough. He forces the issue, demanding that Joab broker a meeting between father and son. No one knows what will happen. It could be a stern, formal encounter between a demanding king and guilty son or a loving father greeting a long lost prodigal son. The courtiers held their breath as they watched. Absalom *came in and bowed down* with his face to the ground before the king. And the king kissed Absalom* (2 Samuel 14:33 NIV). David received his son with forgiveness and grace. I'm sure he believed that Absalom was changed and back in the proper family relationship.

So Absalom is home and the exile is over. "Long live the king and his new crown prince!" At this point in many tales of yore, you'd get the line that says, "and they lived happily ever after." Sadly, this isn't the way David's story goes. Picture his son this way:

> *In all Israel there was not a man so highly praised for his handsome appearance as Absalom. From the top of his head to the sole of his foot there was no blemish in him. Whenever he cut the hair of his head—he used to cut his hair from time to time when it became too heavy for him—he would weigh it, and its weight was two hundred shekels by the royal standard.* (2 Samuel 14:25–26 NIV1984)

That's five pounds. Talk about thick hair! This young fellow is the Fabio of ancient Israel. Yet locks of love they were not. Absalom was vain, egotistical, cunning, and enormously ambitious. He used his handsome looks to launch a campaign to dethrone his father.

SCHEME TO OVERTHROW DAVID

Like something out of today's politics, Absalom pulls together an election team of fifty men who go to the streets throughout Israel, grandstanding Absalom as the alternative candidate to lead them. "The government is broken," they said in effect. "We need an outsider." Following close behind them, Absalom offered himself as an alternative to the king. Many citizens believed him, *so Absalom stole the hearts of the people of Israel* (2 Samuel 15:6).

Absalom doesn't just want their hearts. He wants his father's throne, so he takes the next step: He tells David that he needs to go back to his birthplace in Hebron to worship, fulfilling a vow that he made in exile. David trusts that Absalom is telling the truth, but he's lying. He takes a small army with him along with David's chief military counselor, Ahithophel. With this defection, *the conspiracy grew in strength, and the people with Absalom kept increasing* (2 Samuel 15:12). Hebron is the capital of Judah and the place where David began his reign as king, so it has great historical significance. Once there, Absalom declares himself king and trumpets the message throughout the land.

Word comes to David that all Israel is with Absalom. That is an exaggeration, but the revolution is real. Instead of fighting from the capital, David chooses to flee after he has several strategic conversations.

The priests Zadok and Abiathar are packing up the ark, thinking that they should go with David, but he has them stay in Jerusalem. These men can be more valuable as his spies, sending messages to him through their sons.

David hears that Ahithophel has betrayed him. This is chilling news. He knows that Ahithophel is a brilliant advisor and fears that with his insight, Absalom is assured of victory. As when Jesus was betrayed, David goes to the Mount of Olives, where he weeps and prays to God, *"Turn the counsel of Ahithophel into foolishness"* (2 Samuel 15:31). At the summit he finds his best friend Hushai, an advisor on par with Ahithophel. He has torn his robe, weeping about the unfolding coupe d'etat, so he immediately pledges his loyalty to David and asks to go with him. Instead, David instructs Hushai to stay behind and become one of Absalom's advisors, in reality serving as another spy. In an impressive few hours, David puts together an effective intelligence force to infiltrate his son's inner circle.

Then David flees to the River Jordan, crosses over, and makes camp. David is now the one in exile.

On the heels of David's departure, Absalom and his army arrive with swords drawn, ready to take Jerusalem. They walk into a ghost town. The place is largely deserted except for the priests Zadok and Abiathar with the Ark, David's concubines, and Hushai shouting, *"Long live the king! Long live the king!"* (2 Samuel 16:16). Absalom is surprised Hushai didn't go with his friend, but accepts Hushai's pledge of loyalty.

BATTLE FOR THE THRONE

Having taken Jerusalem without a fight, Absalom doesn't really know what to do next, so he asks Ahithophel for advice. Just as David feared, Ahithophel gives brilliant political advice, even if it sounds morally repulsive to us. The first thing he says is, "Act like the king. Sleep with all of David's concubines in sight of all of Israel." (2 Samuel 16:20–23).

In ancient times, conquering kings would seize all of the previous king's symbols of power as a show of domination. Ahithophel is simply advising Absalom to do what every conquering king did. But it is also fulfilling prophecy. Remember what God said through Nathan about the consequences of David's taking Bathsheba? They would lose the child born in their illicit affair and *"I will raise up trouble against you from within your own house…and he shall lie with your wives in the sight of this very sun"* (2 Samuel 12:11). Absalom is fulfilling this prophecy by sleeping with the concubines.

The second thing Ahithophel suggests is a quick and decisive defeat of David. While Absalom is occupied with the concubines, Ahithophel will take command of 12,000 men and set out in hot pursuit of David. He intends to kill David, but spare the others with him. Thus, he'd make the king's overthrow complete without collateral damage. It was a brilliant strategy, what David feared the most, what he prayed on the Mount of Olives that God would not allow to happen.

When Absalom asks Hushai what he thinks of the plan, Hushai insists that Ahithophel has dangerously underestimated David. The old king is a tough, seasoned guerilla warrior who spent years hiding out from King Saul. David will be fighting mad and ready for them. So Hushai recommends taking time to gather a bigger army, then prepare for one big battle with Absalom himself leading the troops (2 Samuel 17:5–14).

Absalom takes Hushai's advice. At that moment, David's prayer is answered, *For the LORD had ordained to defeat the good counsel of Ahithophel, so that the LORD might bring ruin on Absalom* (2 Samuel 17:14). Hushai isn't just a friend of David's; he is an agent of God. God is using him for a larger purpose, not just to put David back on the throne but to insure that whoever follows David will be a worthy heir of the throne.[16]

Time was what David needed, and Absalom's decision gives it to him. David regroups at Mahanaim as men from all over Israel arrive to offer their support. Kings from other nations send troops; rich benefactors send supplies. David divides the army into three units. He wants to go with them into battle, but his generals decide that he is needed more in the marshalling yard, supporting the troops. They can't risk losing him.

> *So the king stood at the side of the gate, while all the army marched out by hundreds and by thousands. The king ordered Joab and Abishai and Ittai, saying, "Deal gently for my sake with the young man Absalom." And all the people heard when the king gave orders to all the commanders concerning Absalom.*
> (2 Samuel 18:4b–5)

It's a tragic scene. David is impossibly conflicted. Is he a king or father? David is one of the most fabled warriors in scripture, a military giant at one of the most important battles in his life, and now he is saying, "Don't hurt Absalom." He wants the coup to be settled decisively but without harming Absalom. It is an impossible mission.

If David's plea is a prayer, it will not be answered because God has already answered another prayer. He has ordained the shape of the battle *so that the* LORD *might bring ruin on Absalom* (2 Samuel 17:14).

The battle begins. It is a slaughter. Twenty thousand men of Absalom are defeated by David's army. (So much for limiting the collateral damage!) Absalom jumps on his mule and takes off, *and the mule went under the thick branches of a great oak. His head caught fast in the oak, and he was left hanging between heaven and earth, while the mule that was under him went on* (2 Samuel 18:9–10).

There he is, caught perhaps by that Fabio-esque hair, "hanging between heaven and earth." Doesn't that phrase say it all? Absalom is suspended between life and death, between being royal traitor and being a loyal son, between the punishment that should be meted out by the king and the gracious yearning of his father.[17] If you could write the ending of this story, what would it be? Thumbs up or down?

One of Joab's men sees him and reports it to the general. "You didn't kill him?" Joab asks.

"Are you kidding? You heard what the king said. Be gentle with Absalom."

> *Joab said, "I will not waste time like this with you." He took three spears in his hand and thrust them into the heart of Absalom while he was still alive in the oak. And ten young men, Joab's armor-bearers, surrounded Absalom and struck him, and killed him.* (2 Samuel 18:14–15)

Do you make the connection with Joab from a previous chapter in our story? Joab is the one David used to murder Uriah, Bathsheba's husband. Now he is the agent who takes Absalom's life against David's wishes. As he did before, he sends a message to David with word of the victory. David watches from the city and sees the runner coming. As he approaches David, the runner says,

> *"Good tidings for my lord the king! For the LORD has vindicated you this day, delivering you from the power of all who rose up against you." The king said to the Cushite, "Is it well with the young man Absalom?" The Cushite answered, "May the enemies of my lord the king, and all who rise up to do you harm, be like that young man."*

> *The king was deeply moved, and went up to the chamber over the gate, and wept; and as he went, he said, "O my son Absalom, my son, my son Absalom! Would I had died instead of you, O Absalom, my son, my son!"* (2 Samuel 18:31–33)

David's grief is so intense that we can feel it physically. Surely many grieved that day; many unnamed sons were lost, sons who were more loved and had better character than Absalom. But we see David's grief, and it is deep and painfully messy.

Grief always is. There are always unresolved issues, unsaid things, wishes for more time. Such feelings are present in every death, but when the life of a loved one is violently taken, it is more painful; and if the loss is a child, even more so.

PARALYZED BY GRIEF

David is paralyzed by his grief. Grief can do that and we must rely upon others to get us through, to give us the strength to move forward. Oddly, Joab is the one whom God sends to David. He insists that David must make a public appearance as king. Focusing only on his personal loss was putting at risk the restoration of the kingdom. The troops will desert David if they are not publically appreciated, if they do not get a signal that their risk for the country mattered more than the death of a traitor.

David obeys Joab, makes an appearance, and the people are reassured. Life will go on. Long live the king. But long will live the grief too. It will linger for the rest of his life. It always does. We mourn a short time but grieve a lifetime. Relationships do not end with death; they live on in the absence of those we lose, no matter how good or how difficult.

David continues on, but something in him has died. We can see this in his Psalms, which we consider in the next chapter. Despite his best intentions, David could not spare his son from the consequences of his folly, so he experienced profound sorrow.

Sorrow is inevitable when we lose someone we love. It is impossible to have relationships without conflict, love without loss, life without death. It is impossible for us as it was certainly impossible for David. Grief is messy and no one is exempt from it—not you, not me, not even the most powerful man of his time and the man after God's heart, David.

Discussion Questions

1. Absalom was a vain and ambitious young man. Why do you suppose so many people followed him?

2. David proves to be a shrewd fellow by lining up several spies before he leaves Jerusalem. Where had he learned the art of palace intrigue?

3. David's friend Hushai was one of his undercover agents. Why did Absalom favor his advice over Ahithophel's?

4. What's your impression of Joab? How would you describe his character?

5. Pastor Spleth says, "Reconciliation can be slow and painful, especially when families have tragic losses to overcome." Do you need to be reconciled with someone in your family? Would you share this need with your study group?

6. Do you agree with the statement that "it is impossible to have relationships without conflict, love without loss"? Why or why not?

7. If it's true, what should you expect to happen in your family?

8. What counsel would you give to David or anyone who's grieving over the death of a loved one who has betrayed them?

For Further Study

1. David's grief over Absalom caused him to be *ambivalent:* He couldn't decide whether to kill the rebellious crown prince or spare his life. Which of Absalom's actions caused this paralyzing grief? (Read 2 Samuel 13; 15:13–33.)

2. The soldier who found Absalom caught in an oak faced a similar dilemma. What did he fear might happen if he killed the prince—and if he didn't? (Read 2 Samuel 18:10–13.)

3. General Joab did not hesitate to kill Absalom (2 Samuel 18:14–17), even though he had convinced David to let him return from exile just a few years earlier. Why didn't he feel a moral dilemma about this? What do you think changed Ahab's attitude toward Absalom?

WHAT DAVID SAW IN GOD'S HEART
2 Samuel 23:1–5a

Most Americans have read Anne Frank's, *The Diary of a Young Girl*, which is #30 on a list of best-selling books of all time.[18] The diary is an important literary form, ranking right up there with romance, biography, and political memoirs. So, let's take a look at David's diary, the Book of Psalms. Granted, Psalms doesn't fit our modern idea of a diary. The book is not in strict chronological order, and David didn't sit down each day to write something about what he ate or what the weather was like. Nonetheless, in poetry and song, this is where David recorded his most intimate thoughts and feelings about the events of his life.

He wrote a lot of poetry. In the Bible, 74 of the 150 Psalms are attributed to David; but in 1954, among the Dead Sea Scrolls discovered in the caves of Qumran, scholars found a list suggesting that the total number of David's songs and poems was 4,050. If that's true, we don't even have two percent of what David wrote.[19]

We find other poetic pages out of David's diary in 2 Samuel 22:22–23, where David's biographer inserted them. Second Samuel 22 is almost identical to Psalm 18, while the material in chapter 23 is unique. Although the biographer says, *"These are the last words of David"* (2 Samuel 23:1), they are more like a last will and testament that David wrote in anticipation of his death. He isn't on his deathbed with family coming in to see him. (We'll see that in the next chapter.) Rather, David is looking back over his life and trying to make sense of it—ordering things, affirming things, and perhaps even putting some spin on the way he wants to be remembered.

HOW HE WANTS TO BE REMEMBERED

This is the business of the end of life. I can't tell you the number of times, when preparing a memorial service for someone, that I have been handed a piece of paper and told, "Mom wrote this down three years ago," or, "Dad wrote this in 2007 when we first discovered his cancer." It shouldn't surprise us that David is doing this because, we are told, *David grew weary* (2 Samuel 21:15).

We sensed it in the previous chapter as David grieved the death of his son Absalom. The generals wouldn't let him go to war with Absalom's rebel army, preferring that he stay back in the safety of their fortress. At sixty, David wasn't the feared warrior he once was. Then, when he learned of his son's death, he cried out some of the most painful words of scripture: *O my son Absalom! My son, my son Absalom! If only I had died instead of you—O Absalom, my son, my son!* (2 Samuel 18:33). David continues performing the duties of state, but something in him has died, and the events that follow add weight to his tired shoulders.

When David reclaims the throne after Absalom's death, there is a brief and bloody uprising against him, led by a troublemaker named Sheba. He sought to pull the tribes of Israel away from David's rule. This is followed by a terrible three-year famine, which is blamed on David for his failure to punish the blood-stained house of his predecessor, King Saul (2 Samuel 21:1). Then there is a war with the Philistines, in which David tries to lead his army into battle and almost dies. After that, *David's men swore to him, "You shall not go out with us to battle any longer, so that you do not quench the lamp of Israel"* (2 Samuel 21:17).

We don't know how long after this frightening experience in battle that David sits down and begins to write his last words. It might have been a day or two, perhaps a year or two. The content of these poems indicates they were written more than three years after the death of Absalom, probably more. David is likely in his mid- to late-sixties, which makes him a very old man in the tenth century BC. He is losing his physical vitality, perhaps thinking he doesn't have much time left, when he sits down and writes:

> *The LORD is my rock, my fortress, and my deliverer,*
> > *my God, my rock, in whom I take refuge,*
> *my shield and the horn of my salvation,*
> > *my stronghold and my refuge,*
> > *my savior; you save me from violence.*
> *I call upon the LORD, who is worthy to be praised,*
> > *and I am saved from my enemies.* (2 Samuel 22:2–4)

It is not surprising that David believes this. He'd had more lives than the proverbial cat. He should have died when he faced the giant Goliath. He dodged several palace attempts on his life by King Saul. He faced the Philistines over and over again in battle and single-handedly took on two hundred men to win the hand of Michal. (How many times does one man take on 200 and survive?) He had run for his life with Saul's troops in hot pursuit. He foolishly sought refuge from the Philistines and barely escaped death by acting insane. Notice, all of these events took place before he became king. Once he took the throne, he expanded the reach of Israel through countless bloody wars with the Philistines and Ammonites. There were three awful civil wars. David really did *walk through the valley of the shadow of death* (Psalm 23:4 KJV), and not just as a young shepherd boy. A year didn't go by—sometimes a day didn't go by—that he didn't walk through that "valley." He knows ever-present danger confronting him, yet he knows the Lord is with him.

David's last words acknowledge this. They might be paraphrased this way: "I have faith in God. God has been there throughout my life. God is my rock. I called, I cried. God heard. God is the God who comes to the rescue. The God of Israel is faithful and attentive, available and can be summoned into situations where life is in jeopardy."[20] It is an incredible statement of faith, acknowledging that God is present throughout all the circumstance of life, not just when life is good but also when life is very difficult.

Perhaps you say the same thing. Through the many years of being a pastor, I have heard people affirm, over and over again—in life's toughest circumstances and most dangerous moments, even when their lives were threatened—that they knew God's deliverance. They have said, "God sustained me. God watched over me. God gave me the strength to survive." Their words echo what David says here. Perhaps you have said something like this. I know I have many times.

DAVID'S SELF-IMAGE IN LIGHT OF GOD'S BLESSING

I suspect you haven't said what follows, however. In fact, when you read what David says, it might bother you. After David affirms God's providence and powerful protection over the many years of his life, he says,

> *For I have kept the ways of the* LORD,
>> *and have not wickedly departed from my God.*
> *For all his ordinances were before me,*
>> *and from his statutes I did not turn aside.*
> *I was blameless before him,*
>> *and I kept myself from guilt.* (2 Samuel 22:22–24)

You've got to be kidding, David. What's up with this? Is this really who you think you are? As you look back on your life, can you honestly say that you have been good and righteous, a man who never broke the Law? What about all those marriages that God told you not to have? What about committing adultery with your neighbor's wife and then covering it up by murdering him? Haven't you forgotten something? It's astonishing and, frankly, a little hard to swallow.

Some have suggested that David was trying to influence how people perceived him so that he would be remembered more positively. Today, we'd call that putting "spin" on his story. Politicians often do that today. We prefer to remember President Richard Nixon's contributions in foreign policy, especially by opening up relations with China, instead of his shame over the Watergate scandal. When Jimmy Carter shared the news of his cancer diagnosis in the summer of 2015, news analysts reminded us of what a terrific humanitarian and dedicated Christian he is. That's a better life legacy than his challenges with oil embargo and the Iranian hostage crisis while he was President. Perhaps David hoped that future generations would overlook his sin and remember him more positively. But they didn't. In 1 Kings 15:5, we read, *David did what was right in the sight of the* LORD, *and did not turn aside from anything that he commanded him all the days of his life, except in the matter of Uriah the Hittite.* That's a big exception, don't you think?

It is hard to rationalize how David could write about his own purity and righteousness, saying, "I am blameless," unless we put that statement in the context of the incredible faithfulness of God. David is blameless only because of God's generous grace. Any claim of moral legitimacy, merit, or virtue must be heard within the framework of David's confessional diary and God's promise never to take his love away from David.

When the prophet Nathan confronted him with that "matter of Uriah the Hittite," David immediately confessed. He prayed to God and wrote in his diary:

Have mercy on me, O God, according to your steadfast love;
according to your abundant mercy blot out my transgressions....

Create in me a clean heart, O God, and put a new and right
spirit within me.
Do not cast me away from your presence,
and do not take your holy spirit from me.
Restore to me the joy of your salvation,
and sustain in me a willing spirit. (Psalm 51:1, 10–12)

When David wrote his last words, he believed that the "right and willing spirit" was in him and his transgressions were "blotted out." That could only come through the incredible faithfulness in God.[21]

After writing his "I'm blameless" statement, David seems to realize that he has gone overboard in his pietistic self-congratulation. So he acknowledges that while he has accomplished incredible things, God deserves the credit. Even though David looks like a super hero—God enabled him to crush a troop of soldiers, leap over a wall, pursue and destroy his enemies—David readily acknowledges that it is God who gave him life's victories.

It is a wonderful affirmation and we can see why 2 Samuel 22 is largely repeated in Psalm 18. The Book of Psalms has an inscription that says it was written much earlier. Maybe so, and David's biographer decided to use it with another short poem found in 2 Samuel 23. But just maybe, David reread the psalm and decided to add the seven verses that appear in 2 Samuel. If so, I believe he was inspired by the Spirit of God to add them:

> *The God of Israel has spoken, the Rock of Israel has said to me: One who rules over people justly, ruling in the fear of God, is like the light of morning, like the sun rising on a cloudless morning, gleaming from the rain on the grassy land.*
>
> *Is not my house like this with God? For he has made with me an everlasting covenant, ordered in all things and secure.*
> (2 Samuel 23:3–5)

David, inspired by the Holy Spirit, looks to the future and believes it is bright with promise. The future he imagines isn't the kingdom, which he will pass on to his son Solomon, or the one his grandson will receive from Solomon. He is looking centuries into the future. He couldn't possibly imagine such a future without the help of the Holy Spirit; it was too far out and frankly too unbelievable for him to comprehend. But he sees a future descendant, another king to whom God will give his throne. David embraces this everlasting covenant poetically, seeing it as a bright light on the sunrise of the morning, a brilliant sky after the dark clouds of a storm. It's like he's describing Easter, and well it should because this future descendant's name is Jesus. The angel promised Mary, *"He will be great, and will be called the Son of the Most High, and the Lord God will give to him the throne of his ancestor David. He will reign over the house of Jacob forever, and of his kingdom there will be no end"* (Luke 1:32–33). It truly is an everlasting covenant that God has created—eternal, without end. What an incredible legacy, filled with the grace of God's covenant with us, first established with David!

SEEING OURSELVES AS GOD DOES

You may be surprised by this "last will and testament" of David because the last few chapters of David's story have been nothing short of disheartening. I agree. It's hard to watch a giant fall. But even though he did some awful, evil things, David never stopped believing in God. He always returned to God and confessed his sin. God honored his repentance because God is faithful. When God enters into a covenant with us, He keeps His word.

I wonder, if you were to write a last will and testament for your loved ones, what would you say? I cannot imagine writing, "I have been blameless before God and kept myself from sin." But perhaps we need to take a clue from David, for that is the way God sees us through Jesus Christ. As followers of Jesus Christ, when we confess our sins, we are blameless before God; our guilt is put aside because Jesus has made an everlasting covenant with us. There would be nothing greater to claim with your last words. For that matter, there is nothing greater for you to claim today. Our covenant with God through Jesus Christ is the very thing that can give you life, whether the day is like walking through a valley of death or greeting a beautiful sunrise on a cloudless morning.

David saw himself through God's loving eyes. I like that. In the long run, we should all try to see ourselves through God's eyes and not our own. We have failed and been forgiven. We have fallen and been redeemed. Claim that today. If you do, you can say like David,

> *The LORD is my rock, my fortress, and my deliverer,*
> *my God, my rock, in whom I take refuge,*
> *my shield and the horn of my salvation,*
> *my stronghold and my refuge,*
> *my savior.* (2 Samuel 22:2–3a)

Discussion Questions

1. Do you think David was just trying to put a positive "spin" on his reputation, or did he genuinely believe that his life had glorified God? Cite his statements or actions that support your opinion.

2. If your spouse or children came across your daily journal, what would it reveal to them about your relationship with God?

3. David's life demonstrates that "God is present throughout all the circumstance of life, not just when life is good but also when life is very difficult." List some events that showed God was with David in both good and difficult times.

4. Do members of your group disagree about which times were good for David? Then discuss why you see these events differently.

5. Describe the spiritual legacy you leave for your family and friends. What have they learned from your life?

6. Do you see yourself through God's loving eyes? How might that change your opinion of yourself?

For Further Study

1. God's promise of an eternal kingdom applied to David, whose own reign was flawed in so many ways, because the promise was based upon God's grace rather than David's faithfulness. Summarize 2 Peter 3:3–9 in your own words.

2. The promise even applied when God allowed the Jews' enemies to take them into exile. Summarize Micah 4:1–7 in your own words.

IF DAVID'S STORY ENDED HERE
1 Kings 2:1–12

We are at the end of David's life. To put it in contemporary terms, David enters hospice care and his royal servants bring in a visiting nurse to attend to his needs. It is recorded this way:

> *King David was old and advanced in years; and although they covered him with clothes, he could not get warm. So his servants said to him, "Let a young virgin be sought for my lord the king, and let her wait on the king, and be his attendant; let her lie in your bosom, so that my lord the king may be warm."* (1 Kings 1:1–2)

This hardly seems conventional according to our twenty-first-century understating of palliative care; however, the narrator quickly points out that even though the young virgin was very beautiful, she simply took care of David. There wasn't sexual intimacy (v 4).

David was seventy years old, which in biblical times was indeed advanced in years. Put aside all of the incredible reports of longevity in the Bible (with Noah living to be 950 years old and Methuselah singing "Auld Lang Syne" 969 times); scholars believe the average biblical life span was somewhere around thirty-five, equivalent to that of classical Rome. That life expectancy was pulled down by infant mortality, so if a male child survived the first year (and half didn't), he could live to be around fifty. This meant that seventy-year-old David was extremely old and everyone knew it. The family was walking around the palace, assuming that it was simply a matter of days before he breathed his last.

If you've waited at the bedside of a dying relative, you know that the best and the worst can show up in families at such a time. It all depends on how healthy or dysfunctional the family is to begin with. At its best, there is a respect for dying and death, which bring families closer. At its worst, families are driven apart by tagging furniture, laying claim to the Colts tickets, or wearing Mom's jewelry before her last breath is drawn. Death is often a mixed blessing for the grieving family and we see this in David's case—even more so because he was the king.

Who would be the next king? This is early in the monarchy of Israel; David is only the second king, and he wasn't the son of the first, King Saul. The prophet Samuel had anointed him. Samuel had died without leaving a clear royal succession plan, even if David's family had an unspoken one. You know how families work. The eldest almost always believes he is the next in line, whether it is to run the family business or assume the throne (birth order implies as much), so this was the thinking of David's eldest son surviving, Adonijah.

WHO'S FIRST?

You will recall that David had nineteen sons by eight wives. His firstborn son, Amnon, was killed by his third-born, Absalom. (The second son simply disappeared from the record.) Then Absalom was killed by General Joab while trying to dethrone his father. If you are quick at math, you know that left sixteen sons and, yes, Adonijah was next. The last of the nineteen sons was Solomon, sired by David with his last wife, Bathsheba.

With this scorecard in hand, it won't surprise you how the succession game begins. While David lies on his deathbed, Adonijah starts walking around the palace, looking for David's crown. He wants to be king, expects to be king, and says to his mother, "I will be king"—even though there is no indication in scripture that David had said anything about this.

The wanna-be king assembles a transition team and it has two powerful names on it: the high priest Abiathar and Joab, general of the national army. These were two of King David's closest advisors and they give Adonijah their full support. He gets a chariot and rides around Jerusalem with fifty men running before him through the streets of Jerusalem, announcing his imminent coronation. He slaughters sheep, cattle, and fattened calves for his inaugural banquet and invites just about every government official and all of his brothers except one—his youngest brother, Solomon. At a place just outside of Jerusalem named En-rogel, the party begins. Even though David is still fogging a mirror, the high priest and the general of the Army are gnawing on lamb chops and shouting, *"Long live King Adonijah!"* (1 Kings 1:25).

It's hard to keep something like that secret. The prophet Nathan hears what is going on. (By the way, he's the one official who didn't receive an invitation to the banquet.) Immediately, he begins a counter conspiracy. He advises Bathsheba to go to the bedside of King David and tell him that he had earlier promised the throne to Solomon. We don't know if he actually had, but Nathan plans to show up while the Bathsheba conversation is going on, to provide support for the succession plan.[22]

Bathsheba makes her case, then Nathan walks in and confirms it. Whether reminded or manipulated, David says, *"I swore to you by the LORD, the God of Israel, 'Your son Solomon shall succeed me as king, and he shall sit on my throne in my place,' so will I do this day"* (1 Kings 1:30). David appoints his own transition team to support Solomon. It includes Nathan, the prophet; Zadok, the second high priest; and one of the national army's most distinguished warriors, Benaiah.

David has them put Solomon on his mule and parade him through town, gathering a crowd along the way. He instructs Zadok to take Solomon to the scared tent with the Ark of the Covenant and anoint Solomon as king. This they do.

When the anointing ceremony is finished, Solomon emerges with oil dripping and crown in place. The palace guard blow their trumpets and people began to shout, "Long live King Solomon! Long live King Solomon!" It grows louder and louder until the ground begins to shake.

Miles away, Adonijah is just picking up his dessert fork to take a bite of cake when Joab asks, "What's all the noise coming from Jerusalem?" Just then, Abiathar's son Jonathan arrives.

Inebriated with the power he thinks he is getting, Adonijah joyfully says, *"Come in, for you are a worthy man and surely you are bringing good news"* (1 Kings 1:42). But no, Jonathan tells him that David has made Solomon king and that the youngest brother is already sitting on the throne.

Can you imagine Adonijah's reaction? He spit out his champagne, dropped his slice of cake, and ran as fast as he could to the altar of God, where he grabbed hold of the horns. This was an ancient way of seeking sanctuary. From the altar, Adonijah begged Solomon not to harm him. (Why would he be afraid of that? Likely, because he had planned to eliminate Solomon! Ancient kings often killed off any potential threats, even if they were family.)

Yet Solomon was not going to rule that way. From the throne, he said, *"If he shows himself to be worthy, not a hair of his head will fall to the ground; but if evil is found in him, he will die"* (1 Kings 1:52 NIV). That's the just way of ruling. Solomon sent men to bring Adonijah to the royal court, where he publicly extended mercy and grace to him. As his first act, King Solomon shows himself to be very wise.

DEATHBED SCENE

We don't know if Solomon walked directly from the throne room in Jerusalem to David's bed or was summoned days later when David's beautiful hospice nurse sensed that his pulse was weakening. But shortly after all the family intrigue, Solomon finds himself at David's bedside.

Because David had written all of his life, I suspect that he had carefully written down the things he wanted to say to Solomon. I wish I could tell you that all of it was wonderful; in fact, his final instructions were a mixed bag. It starts this way:

> *When David's time to die drew near, he charged his son Solomon, saying: "I am about to go the way of all the earth. Be strong, be courageous, and keep the charge of the* L<small>ORD</small> *your God, walking in his ways and keeping his statutes, his commandments, his ordinances, and his testimonies, as it is written in the law of Moses."* (1 Kings 2:1–3)

Isn't that a wonderful deathbed statement? *"Be strong; be a man of God; walk in God's ways."* I can't think of any better advice for a father to give his son. David is speaking with the voice of experience. David had been incredibly close to God and had unshakeable confidence in God to deliver him. Without fear, he had faced numerous enemies and challenges. David had learned that God was his rock, the horn of his salvation. So he told Solomon, *"Live God's way and God's ways are laid out for us in scripture."* That's great advice for any parent to give to a son or daughter. God's Word really is a lamp for our feet and light for our path. (Psalm 119:105).

David adds that Solomon should do this *"so that you may prosper in all that you do and wherever you turn"* (1 Kings 2:3). Walking in God's ways has benefits. My father taught me to do what's right simply because it is the right thing to do. He said I should do the right thing, not because I would get something in return, but because that's who I was meant to be. But David says that following God's Word and living God's way leads to prosperity. It doesn't mean that we are going to get rich. It means that a God-centered life leads to satisfaction and joy; it brings happiness, health, and well-being. Good advice, and it would have been perfect if David died then and there. But that would not have been typical of David's story.

With his dying breath, David continues to give Solomon advice—awful, terrible, bad advice. He names three people he wants Solomon to deal with: Joab, Barzillai and Shimei. *"Now you yourself know what Joab son of Zeruiah did to me"* (1 Kings 2:5a NIV), he said. We know lots of things that Joab did *for* David. He was his commander-in-chief who fought at David's side. He covered up David's affair with Bathsheba, murdered her husband Uriah, and kept David on the throne when Absalom tried to steal it. David would not be the king that he was and Israel would not be the nation it was without the heroism of Joab. But Joab had a dark side, too. He had killed two other commanders of Israel's armies and that angered David.²³ So David says to his son, *"Deal with him according to your wisdom, but do not let his gray head go down to the grave in peace"* (1 Kings 2:6). He sounds like the Godfather giving instructions to a son: "Take him out."

Next on David's list were the sons of Barzillai, the Gileadite, the wealthy and generous benefactor who had supplied David's army when Absalom tried to take his throne. Barzillai was incredibly rich, as rich as a king, so he expected no reward from David for the war aid he provided. David somehow felt obligated and said, *"Let his sons eat at the king's table"* (a sort of euphemism for "Put them on welfare" or, "Make them like family").

Given the perennial conversation about foreign aid in this country, I suspect David's order may have brought a similar response in the ancient world. "Give the rich foreigners aid? You've got to be kidding!"

The final name on David's list is Shimei. A relative of King Saul's, Shimei held a grudge because someone from his family didn't become king. Years earlier, he had cursed King David, called him a scoundrel and a dog. He had thrown stones at him. David said he'd forgiven Shimei for his bad behavior and took an oath not to harm him, but it must have eaten at David. He seemed to be obsessed with the insult he felt. He wants him dead too, so he says, *"But now, do not consider him innocent. You are a man of wisdom; you will know what to do to him. Bring his gray head down to the grave in blood"* (1 Kings 2:9 NIV). It is ghastly advice. Then he dies.

> *Then David slept with his ancestors, and was buried in the city of David. The time that David reigned over Israel was forty years; he reigned seven years in Hebron, and thirty-three years in Jerusalem. So Solomon sat on the throne of his father David; and his kingdom was firmly established.* (1 Kings 2:10–12)

It's a tragic ending but, in an odd sort of way, fitting. David died the way he lived. David was the great king of Israel who united the tribes and built a great nation. He was a master poet and great musician, the "man after God's own heart." He was all of those things and at the same time, he was a deeply flawed human being, a sinner, an adulterer, and a murderer who broke almost all of the commandments at one time or another. He was a violent man who planned violence on his deathbed. Like his life, he offered the best and the worst with his dying breath.

THE BEST AND THE WORST

So concludes the story of the greatest hero of the Old Testament, a man who rose to true greatness but fell like a giant. He was a man after God's own heart who, far too often, didn't act like it. In that way, David was like us. I think most of us really love God but, in the end, we don't do right things.

If that connects with you, then I hope this will too: God can still use you, just as God used David. His true legacy wasn't the kingdom that he created but the kingdom to come, because God indeed had a succession plan in place. Through David, a Son would be given to God's people and the government would be on His shoulders. Through the Son, peace would have no end. This Son would reign on David's throne and over his kingdom, establishing and upholding it with justice and righteousness from that time on and forever. God's hand was upon all of this, for the prophet Isaiah said, *"The zeal of the LORD Almighty will accomplish this"* (Isaiah 9:7 NIV). Who was David's long-awaited successor? You can find His name listed along with David's on the first line of the New Testament. It simply reads, *"an account of the genealogy of Jesus the Messiah, the son of David"* (Matthew 1:1 NIV).

If you have risen to the heights of moral courage and fallen to the depths of moral failure as David did, don't assume that God is finished with you. The old saying goes, "It isn't over till it's over"—but when God is involved, it isn't over even then!

Discussion Questions

1. Bathsheba summons the prophet Nathan to substantiate her claim that David had promised the throne to her son Solomon. Can you recall another time when Nathan confronted David with his responsibility? (2 Samuel 12).

2. If you were writing David's obituary at the time of his death, what accomplishments would you praise? What failures would you acknowledge?

3. If young David (the shepherd boy) could have stepped forward in time to warn old David (the powerful king), what might he have said was most likely to ruin him?

4. Reflect on a time when you fell short of God's standards for holy living. How did you know you had missed the mark? How was your relationship with God restored?

5. We often hear about "fallen giants" in daily news reports—corporate executives who fall into fraud, politicians who fall into lying and sexual sin, even church leaders who fall into corrupt schemes and drug addiction. Based on David's experience, why do you suppose such "giants" are nonetheless liable to fall?

6. What kind of temptation is most likely to trip you—pride, power, money, sex, self-indulgence, or something else? What steps can you take to overcome it?

For Further Study

1. List other heroes and heroines of faith described in the Bible. (If you need a memory prompter, try Hebrews 11.) Beside each one, note a moral failure that person may have experienced.

2. What do these accounts tell you about God's relationship with fallible human beings? What does it tell you about God's relationship with you?

1. Stanley Sprecher, *Radiology*, July 1990, as quoted in *David and Goliath* by Malcolm Gladwell.

2. Malcolm Gladwell, *David and Goliath: Underdogs, Misfits and the Art of Battling Giants* (New York: Little, Brown and Company, 2013), 6.

3. Ibid., 6.

4. Eugene H. Peterson, *A Long Obedience in the Same Direction*, 2nd ed. (Downers Grove, IL: InterVarsity Press, 2000), 54.

5. "Netanyahu Pledges: Jerusalem Never Will Be Divided Again," by Yoni Kempinski, *Arutz Sheva*, May 18, 2015.

6. Quote furnished by the Acton Institute. http://www.acton.org/research/lord-acton-quote-archive, accessed July 7, 2016.

7. Walter Bruggemann, *First and Second Samuel: Interpretation: A Bible Commentary for Teaching and Preaching* (Louisville, KY: Westminster John Knox Press, 2012) 249.

8. Mark Twain, "Letters from the Earth: Letter X." http://www.online-literature.com/twain/letters-from-the-earth/11/, accessed July 7, 2016.

9. T.G. Long, "The Fall of the House of Uzzah...and Other Difficult Preaching Texts." *Journal for Preachers*, 1983, 7:1, 13–19.

10. Brueggemann, 249.

11. "How to Tell the Difference between Love and Lust," post published by Judith Orloff, M.D., *Psychology Today*, August 15, 2011.

12. Brueggemann, 278.

13. Leith Anderson, "Royal Lust," Wooddale Church, August 8, 2010.

14. "The Origin of the Phrase, 'Speaking Truth to Power,'" by John Green. http://classroom.synonym.com/origin-phrase-speaking-truth-power-11676.html, accessed July 8, 2016.

15. Brueggemann, 28.

16. Ibid., 313.

17. Ibid., 319.

18. http://www.listchallenges.com/101-best-selling-books-of-all-time, accessed July 15, 2016.

19. No'am V, "The origin of the list of David's songs in 'David's compositions,'" *Dead Sea Discoveries,* 2006, 13(2):134–49. Available from *ATLASerials*, Religion Collection, Ipswich, MA. Accessed August 17, 2015.

20. Brueggemann, 340.

21. Walter Brueggemann, "2 Samuel 21-24: An Appendix of Deconstruction," *The Catholic Biblical Quarterly*, July 1988; 50(3):383–397. Available from ATLA Serials, Religion Collection.

22. B.O. Long, "A Darkness between Brothers: Solomon and Adonijah," *Journal for The Study of the Old Testament*, 1979: 94.

23. F. Papek, "David's Ambiguous Testament in 1 Kings 2:1-12 and the Role of Joab in the Succession Narrative," *Communio Viatorum*, Vol. 52, No. 1, 4–26.

CPSIA information can be obtained
at www.ICGtesting.com
Printed in the USA
FSOW04n0321041017
39274FS